A Catalog of Multi-Part Repertoire for Wind Instruments or for Undesignated Instrumentation before 1600

Books by David Whitwell

Philosophic Foundations of Education
Foundations of Music Education
Music Education of the Future
The Sousa Oral History Project
The Art of Musical Conducting
The Longy Club: 1900–1917
A Concise History of the Wind Band
Wagner on Bands
Berlioz on Bands
Aesthetics of Music in Ancient Civilizations
Aesthetics of Music in the Middle Ages

The History and Literature of the Wind Band and Wind Ensemble Series

Volume 1 The Wind Band and Wind Ensemble Before 1500
Volume 2 The Renaissance Wind Band and Wind Ensemble
Volume 3 The Baroque Wind Band and Wind Ensemble
Volume 4 The Wind Band and Wind Ensemble of the Classical Period (1750–1800)
Volume 5 The Nineteenth-Century Wind Band and Wind Ensemble
Volume 6 A Catalog of Multi-Part Repertoire for Wind Instruments or for Undesignated Instrumentation before 1600
Volume 7 Baroque Wind Band and Wind Ensemble Repertoire
Volume 8 Classical Period Wind Band and Wind Ensemble Repertoire
Volume 9 Nineteenth-Century Wind Band and Wind Ensemble Repertoire
Volume 10 A Supplementary Catalog of Wind Band and Wind Ensemble Repertoire
Volume 11 A Catalog of Wind Repertoire before the Twentieth Century for One to Five Players
Volume 12 A Second Supplementary Catalog of Early Wind Band and Wind Ensemble Repertoire
Volume 13 Name Index, Volumes 1–12, The History and Literature of the Wind Band and Wind Ensemble

www.whitwellbooks.com

David Whitwell

A Catalog of Multi-Part Repertoire for Wind Instruments or for Undesignated Instrumentation before 1600

THE HISTORY AND LITERATURE OF THE WIND BAND AND WIND ENSEMBLE, VOLUME 6

EDITED BY CRAIG DABELSTEIN

WHITWELL PUBLISHING • AUSTIN, TEXAS, USA

Whitwell Publishing, Austin 78701
www.whitwellbooks.com

© 1983, 2012 by David Whitwell
All rights reserved. First edition 1983.
Second edition 2012

Printed in the United States of America

PAPERBACK
ISBN-13: 1936512351
ISBN-10: 978-1-936512-35-5

All images used in this book are in the public domain except where otherwise noted.

Composed in Bembo Book

Contents

Foreword	vii
Notes on the catalog	xiii
Library Abbreviations	xv
Acknowledgements	xxi

PART 1 FOURTEENTH-CENTURY SOURCES

England   3
    Manuscript Collections Without Instrument Designation

France   3
    Manuscript Collections Without Instrument Designation

The German-Speaking Countries   3
    Manuscript Collections Without Instrument Designation
    Single Title Manuscripts Designated for Winds

Italy   4
    Manuscript Collections Without Instrument Designation

The Low Countries   4
    Manuscript Collections Without Instrument Designation

PART 2 FIFTEENTH-CENTURY SOURCES

Bohemia   7
    Manuscript Collections Without Instrument Designation

England   7
    Manuscript Collections Without Instrument Designation

France and The Low Countries   8
    Manuscript Collections Without Instrument Designation

The German-Speaking Countries   9
    Manuscript Collections Without Instrument Designation
    Works Associated with Maximilian I

Italy   12
    Manuscript Collections Without Instrument Designation
    Print Collections Without Instrument Designation

Poland   17
    Manuscript Collections Without Instrument Designation

Spain and Portugal   18
    Manuscript Collections Without Instrument Designation

Music of the Basse-Dance   18

PART 3 SIXTEENTH-CENTURY SOURCES

Austria — 23
Manuscript Collections Without Instrument Designation
Single Title Prints Designated for Any Instrument

Bohemia — 23
Manuscript Collections Without Instrument Designation

Denmark — 23
Manuscript Collections Without Instrument Designation
Single Title Manuscripts Without Instrument Designation

England — 31
Manuscript Collections Without Instrument Designation
Print Collections Designated for Winds
Print Collections Without Instrument Designation
Single Title Manuscripts Designated for Winds
Single Title Manuscripts Without Instrument Designation

France — 37
Manuscript Collections Designated for Winds
Manuscript Collections Without Instrument Designation
Print Collections Designated for Any Instrument
Single Title Prints Designated for Any Instrument
Single Title Prints Without Instrument Designation

Germany — 57
Manuscript Collections Designated for Winds
Manuscript Collections Without Instrument Designation
Print Collections Designated for Winds
Print Collections Designated for Any Instrument
Print Collections Without Instrument Designation
Single Title Manuscripts Designated for Winds
Single Title Manuscripts Without Instrument Designation
Single Title Prints Designated for Winds
Single Title Prints Without Instrument Designation

Hungary — 79
Manuscript Collections Without Instrument Designation

Italy	79
Manuscript Collections Without Instrument Designation	
Print Collections Designated for Winds	
Print Collections Designated for Any Instrument	
Print Collections Without Instrument Designation	
Single Title Manuscripts Without Instrument Designation	
Single Title Prints Designated for Winds	
Single Title Prints Without Instrument Designation	
The Low Countries	106
Manuscript Collections Without Instrument Designation	
Print Collections Designated for Any Instrument	
Single Title Manuscripts Without Instrument Designation	
Single Title Prints Without Instrument Designation	
Poland	124
Manuscript Collections Without Instrument Designation	
Spain	125
Manuscript Collections Without Instrument Designation	
Switzerland	126
Manuscript Collections Without Instrument Designation	
Index	127
About The Author	137

Foreword

THIS VOLUME IS THE SIXTH, and a companion volume to the first two volumes, in the series, *The History and Literature of the Wind Band and Wind Ensemble*, comprised of the following volumes:

1. The Wind Band and Wind Ensemble before 1500
2. The Renaissance Wind Band and Wind Ensemble
3. The Baroque Wind Band and Wind Ensemble
4. The Classical Period Wind Band and Wind Ensemble
5. The Nineteenth-Century Wind Band and Wind Ensemble
6. A Catalog of Multi-Part Repertoire for Wind Instruments or for Undesignated Instrumentation before 1600
7. Baroque Wind Band and Wind Ensemble Repertoire
8. Classical Period Wind Band and Wind Ensemble Repertoire
9. Nineteenth-Century Wind Band and Wind Ensemble Repertoire
10. A Supplementary Catalog of Early Band and Wind Ensemble Repertoire
11. A Catalog of Wind Repertoire before the Twentieth Century for One to Five Players
12. A Second Supplementary Catalog of Early Wind Band and Wind Ensemble Repertoire
13. Name Index, Volumes 1–12, The History and Literature of the Wind Band and Wind Ensemble

In attempting to identify the repertoire of the Medieval and Renaissance wind bands, one is immediately faced with the fact that before 1600 it is rare to find specific instruments mentioned in the score. We are helped by occasional use of early terms which were generally understood to be references to pure wind bands, such as 'haut,' 'Stark,' 'alta' and, in England, 'Noise.' Similar terms such as 'bas,' 'bajo' and 'still' were designations of ensembles making softer sounds, for use in smaller rooms, and while they were often primarily winds they could have also included some individual string instruments. We also are guided by the fact that recent studies of early civic, church and court records make it safe to say that before 1550 it was the wind player who was the professional musician, while the prototype violinist, the 'beer fiddler,' was for the most part a wandering amateur playing for handouts. And where there were individual string players employed by a court they performed as individuals and not as a voice in a larger ensemble.

But these studies of civic, church and court records are relatively recently published and in the absence of these records the views of earlier musicologists interested in questions of early ensemble performance accompanying singers included a certain prejudice against instrumentalists in general and against wind instruments in particular. Some of this prejudice had its basis in early iconography in which it was noticed that singers were pictured holding music while instrumentalists were only very rarely pictured with music, the inference being that the instrumentalists pictured could not read music and were not performing together with the singers. But surely most scholars today would agree that this was only a matter of identification. A person on canvas cannot be identified as a singer unless he is holding music, whereas it is the instrument itself which identifies the instrumentalist as being a musician.

This residual prejudice can be seen in the judgment of various scholars even in those cases where one voice in a score was clearly designated for an instrument. Consider, for example, the disagreement with respect to nine early church compositions which appear to have a part intended to be played by a trumpet.

1. First, there is a three-part *Chanson*, 'J'aime bien celuy qui s'en va,' by Pierre Fontaine, in which a part is marked, 'Contratenor Trompette,' replacing an earlier contratenor part. Thibault, Wangermee, and Marix all accept this part as having been intended for performance on a trumpet.[1] Harrison, on the other hand, after an analysis of the probable technical limits of the early slide-trumpet, believes the part could not have been played on a trumpet and must have been intended for vocalization 'in the style of a trumpet.'[2] Munrow believed that this part was actually intended for the sackbut, suggesting further that it was 'added almost certainly by Guillaume Dufay in 1434 or 1435.'[3]

[1] G. Thibault, 'Le Concert Instrumental au XVe Siècle,' in Jean Jacquot, ed., *La Musique Instrumentale de la Renaissance* (Paris: Editions du CNRS, 1955), 29; Robert Wangermée, *Flemish Music and Society in the Fifteenth and Sixteenth Centuries* (New York: Praeger, 1968), 200; and Jeanne Marix, *Histoire de la Musique et des Musiciens de la Court de Bourgogne sous le regne de Philippe le Bon* (Strasbourg: Heitz, 1939), 105.

[2] Frank L. Harrison, 'Tradition and Innovation in Instrumental Usage 1100–1450,' in *Aspects of Medieval and Renaissance Music* (New York: Norton, 1966), 331ff.

[3] David Munrow, *Instruments of the Middle Ages and Renaissance* (London: Oxford University Press, 1976), 20.

2. An isorhythmic *Motet*, 'Ave Virgo lux Maria,' by Franchois, begins with a forty-two measure 'introitus' in three-parts, the lowest of which is marked, 'Trumpetta Introitus.' Reese saw this as an almost separate composition, differing in structure from the vocal portion, in which at least the lowest part was to be played by a slide-trumpet.[4] Harrison again rejects this possibility, arguing for vocalization.[5]
3. In the 'Gloria' of a *Mass* by Arnoldus de Latins, one finds a contratenor part marked, 'Tuba sub fuga.' Munrow again believed this was rather for sackbut, while Harrison now believes the part was truly playable by a trumpet.[6]
4. A *Mass* by Estienne Grossin, lacking only an 'Agnus,' has a contratenor part designated for slide-trumpet, according to Reese.[7] Harrison and Caldwell tend to agree it was in fact intended for the trumpet.[8]
5. The best known of these examples is the three-part 'Et in terra,' of Dufay, which has a lower part designated, 'ad modum tubae,' and seems to be generally accepted as having been intended for the trumpet.
6. Harrison mentions an *Antiphon*, 'Virgo dulcis,' by Henry of Lauffenberg, which has a part marked for trumpet which he again believes only means vocalization in the style of a trumpet.[9]
7. Ehmann mentions a 'Missa tubae' and 'Kyrie tubae' by Jean Cousin, found in the Trient Codices (I:TRa 90 and 93), which he seems to identify with the trumpet.[10] Grove is somewhat more guarded, stating, 'The name is derived from the melodic style of the tenor and contratenor parts which are written in the manner of trumpet music and which may have been intended for performance by slide-trumpets.'[11]
8. Thibault mentions a Motet, 'Virgo Dulcis,' by Henri de Fribourg, for voice and two 'tubae.'[12] He also mention a three-part, 'Tuba Gallicalis,' which is contained in the same source,[13] for three sackbuts. Harrison suggests that only the middle part of this work could be played on the trumpet, in spite of the title.[14]

[4] Gustave Reese, *Music in the Renaissance* (New York: Norton, 1959), 42.

[5] Harrison, 'Tradition and Innovation in Instrumental Usage 1100–1450.'

[6] Munrow, *Instruments of the Middle Ages and Renaissance*, and Harrison, 'Tradition and Innovation in Instrumental Usage 1100–1450.'

[7] Reese, *Music in the Renaissance*, 43.

[8] Harrison, 'Tradition and Innovation in Instrumental Usage 1100–1450,' and John Caldwell, *Medieval Music* (Bloomington: Indiana University Press, 1978), 234.

[9] Harrison, 'Tradition and Innovation in Instrumental Usage 1100–1450.'

[10] Wilhelm Ehmann, *Tibilustrium* (Kassel: Bärenreiter, 1950), 157–158.

[11] George Grove, *The New Grove Dictionary of Music and Musicians*. Edited by Stanley Sadie. (London: Macmillan, 1980). V, 4.

[12] Thibault, 'Le Concert Instrumental au XVe Siècle.'

[13] Strasbourg, Bibliothèque du Conservatoire (MS. 222'.C.22), now lost.

[14] Harrison, 'Tradition and Innovation in Instrumental Usage 1100–1450.'

9. Finally, Munrow mentions a 'Virgo dulcis,' by Henricus de Libero Castro, with a tenor marked, 'Laudate cum in sono tube,' and a contratenor marked, 'Tube.' Munrow again suggests, for technical reasons, that the sackbut was actually intended.[15]

[15] Munrow, *Instruments of the Middle Ages and Renaissance*, 68.

These examples of the use of instruments being used together with singers in the church may represent a tradition older than we yet assume. Reaney mentions one medieval writer who indicated that as early as the thirteenth century instruments were used in the upper voices of organum.[16] In Grove one reads, 'minstrels seem to have played the tenor and contratenor parts of the standard three-voice polyphonic chanson of the 14th century.'[17]

[16] Gilbert Reaney, 'The Performance of Medieval Music,' in *Aspects of Medieval and Renaissance Music* (New York: Norton, 1966), 707. Although rarely acknowledged, more than one early writer used the very word *organum* as a synonym for instruments.

It was this same lack of information later to be found in the civic, church and court records which greatly troubled early musicologists regarding the vast extant repertoire of multi-part vocal music, sacred and secular, in which the text is not found in all voices. Sometime the text is found in only the upper voice, with the three lower voices having only musical notes but with an incipit of text[18] or no text at all, sometimes two voices with text and two without and sometimes three voices with text and one without. The early musicologists did not seem to assign any significance to the fact that the voices without text often looked quite different, rhythmically, than the voices with text. Even in those cases where the non-text voice consisted of very long tones, the early musicologists preferred to believe that in those voices the singers just manipulated the text from the upper voice to create a new vocal line. Left unanswered was why the composer or scribe did not bother to write in the text.

[17] Grove, 12:348.

[18] In the tenor part of Kyrie II of Gheerkin's *Missa Panis quem ego dabo* in the manuscript Cambrai 124, the scribe drew a three-man wind ensemble playing at the bottom of a part with occasional fragments of text for the purpose of helping the instrumentalist coordinate his performance against the upper voices with text.

Some early musicologists took the position that the singers knew the texts from memory and could therefore 'vocalize' an improvisation over the given notes. But in the case of the large chansonniers or in collections such as the *Odhecaton* prints (1501), the suggestion that singers knew the texts for hundreds of polyphonic works in several languages by memory seems quite beyond belief.

Today, finally, most musicologists have come to understand that these textless lines were performed by instruments as perhaps a few examples will suffice.

Often the superius and tenor have text, while the wordless contratenor is obviously instrumental.[19]

Almost always (they were) written for three voices, but only the topmost one was meant to be sung, the two others being instrumental.

......

In Dufay's time, ballades, rondeaux and chansons were most often composed for three voices, a principal voice which was sung plus, below it, tenor and counter-tenor parts intended to be played by instruments.[20]

At all events the consensus still seems to be that such parts without text are instrumental, and the variety of instruments to be found in the 14th and 15th centuries suggests that these were used for playing the accompanied songs which sprang up at very much the same time.[21]

When ensemble music began to be published, the title page often included the phrase 'or any instruments,' no doubt in part to expand the potential for sales. Should such a score be considered as a wind band score? One must not judge on the basis of clefs, because the wind players were adept with all clefs. Even the eye is a risky judge, for there are eighteenth- and nineteenth-century oboe scores which are fully as technically difficult as violin parts of the same period. In this case range is a clue, as the oboe did not descend as low as the violin. In the end one could make complex judgments based on style but the fact is that the early composer did not yet pay much attention to this question. Even Mozart made no objections when an orchestra with no flutes wanted to perform his 'Paris' Symphony. As long as someone played the parts, he was happy.

To help answer this question the reader may recall that it is generally accepted that before original instrumental ensemble music appeared in substantial quantities, these players took polyphonic vocal compositions and transcribed them, or played them at sight, as their repertoire. That being the case, they probably looked toward almost all polyphonic vocal music for this purpose, certainly all secular music. As Brown points out, 'There is scarcely any vocal music at all that cannot be played on instruments and that was not so performed.'[22] As he suggests, there was a great deal of vocal polyphony published during the sixteenth century which does not carry this phrase, yet is also playable by instruments. Perhaps, therefore, those prints which do carry this recommendation for instrumental performance are indeed those which we may assume

[19] Reese, *Music in the Renaissance*, 54, on the music of Dufay.

[20] Wangermée, *Flemish Music and Society in the Fifteenth and Sixteenth Centuries*, 122, 213, in the chansons of Binchois.

[21] Otto Gombosi, 'About Dance and Dance Music in the Late Middle Ages,' *The Musical Quarterly* (1941): 289.

[22] Howard Mayer Brown, *Instrumental Music Printed Before 1600* (Cambridge, MA: Harvard University Press, 1965), 3.

were most likely performed by early instrumental groups. We know that when civic wind bands first begin to play public concerts, they played motets and chansons. Perhaps some of their literature was taken from these works in question, which have been included in this catalog.

Finally, because my purpose is to identify the possible literature of the early wind bands, those sixteenth-century ensemble works which were specifically designated for either strings (usually plucked) or keyboard have not been included.

While volumes 7–12 are compiled primarily on the basis of my own research in libraries in Europe, the present volume contains much information found in the following concordances.

> Howard Mayer Brown, *Instrumental Music Printed Before 1600* (Cambridge, MA: Harvard University Press, 1965).
> George Grove, *The New Grove Dictionary of Music and Musicians*. Edited by Stanley Sadie. (London: Macmillan, 1980), 17:590ff for manuscripts and 17:702ff for prints.
> *Census-Catalogue of Manuscript Sources of Polyphonic Music 1400–1550* (Stuttgart: American Institute of Musicology, 1979), two volumes of which were published by 1983.

David Whitwell
Austin, Texas

Notes on the Catalog

THE MANUSCRIPTS given in the following catalog are listed under the country represented by the literature in the manuscript or where it was copied, which carries the implication the music was performed there. In other words, the manuscripts are not listed under the countries in which the manuscripts are currently deposited. In the interval since this catalog was first published in 1983 there has been a reunification of Germany with the result that the old R.I.S.M. library symbols have been changed and indeed in many cases the music has been moved to the *Staatsbibliothek* in Berlin. In this catalog, however, we retain the old R.I.S.M. symbols and shelf-mark because even in those cases where the music has been moved to a new location the old information is necessary for the new library to identify these specific manuscripts for those who may want copies today.

Beyond this, the manuscripts are listed in chronological order, in so far as this can be determined. The information given here represents that which was known in 1983. It may be expected that new studies and new information has been added in the subsequent 30 years. The reader can search on line using the library R.I.S.M. symbol and shelf-mark and in most cases can be immediately provided with the present state of knowledge concerning a particular manuscript.

The printed material is listed alphabetically, by composer or publisher. Unless 'otherwise indicated, when a library source is given it also means the copy is complete. Where at least one complete copy is extant, no further incomplete sources are given.

The music represented in this catalog has been organized with regard to three basic considerations:

1. whether the music is manuscript or in print,
2. whether the music is contained in a collection or is a single title,
3. whether the music is designated for winds, for 'any instrument,' or without specific designation.

Library Abbreviations for this Catalog

A: Austria

HE	Heiligenkreuz, Zisterzienserstift
Wgm	Wien, Gesellschaft der Musikfreunde in Wien
Wn	Wien, Österreichische Nationalbibliothek

B: Belgium

Bc	Bruxelles, Conservatoire Royal de Musique, Bibliothèque
Br	Bruxelles, Bibliothèque Royale Albert 1er

BRD: West Germany (Bundesrepublik Deutschland)

As	Augsburg, Staats- und Stadtbibliothek
B	Berlin (West), Staatsbibliothek (Stiftung Preussischer Kulturbesitz)
BAa	Bamberg, Staatsarchiv
BE	Berleburg, Fürstlich Sayn-Wittgenstein- Berleburgsche Bibliothek
Bhm	Berlin (West), Staatliche Hochschule für Musik und Darstellende Kunst
DS	Darmstadt, Hessische Landes- und Hochschulbibliothek
F	Frankfurt/Main, Stadt- und Universitätsbibliothek, Musik- und Theaterabteilung Manskopfisches Museum.
Gs	Göttingen, Niedersächsische Staats- und Universitätsbibliothek
HB	Heilbronn, Stadtbücherei, Musiksammlung, mit Gymnasialbibliothek
Hs	Hamburg, Staats- and Universitätsbibliothek, Musikabteilung
HVl	Hanover, Niedersächsische Landesbibliothek
ISL	Iserlohn, Bibliothek Varnhagen
KA	Karlsruhe, Badische Landesbibliothek, Musikabteilung
Kl	Kassel, Murhard'sche Bibliothek der Stadt Kassel und Landesbibliothek
KNu	Köln, Universität- und Stadtbibliothek
Lr	Lüneburg, Ratsbucherei und Stadtarchiv der Stadt Lüneburg, Musikabteilung
LÜh	Lübeck, Bibliothek der Hansestadt Lübeck
Mbs	München, Bayerische Staatsbibliothek, Musiksammlung
Mu	München, Universitätsbibliothek
Ngm	Nürnberg, Bibliothek des Germanischen National- Museums
Nla	Nürnberg, Bibliothek beim Landeskirchlichen Archiv
Nst	Nürnberg, Stadtbibliothek
PA	Paderborn, Erzbischöfliche Akademische Bibliothek

XVIII LIBRARY ABBREVIATIONS

Rp	Regensburg, Bischöfliche Zentralbibliothek
Rtt	Regensburg, Fürstlich Thurn und Taxissche Hofbibliothek
TRs	Trier, Stadtbibliothek
Usch	Ulm, Von Schermar'sche Familienstiftung, Bibliothek
Ud	Ulm, Dombibliothe
W	Wolfenbüttel (Niedersächsen), Herzog-August-Bibliothek, Musikabteilung
WS	Wasserburg/Inn, Chorarchiv St. Jakob, Pfarramt

CH: Switzerland

BU	Burgdorf, Stadtbibliothek
LAcu	Lausanne, Bibliothèque cantonale et universitaire
SAM	Samedan , Biblioteca Fundaziun Planta
SGa	St. Gallen, Staatsarchiv und Kantonsbibliothek
SGs	St. Gallen, Stiftsbibliothek
Zz	Zürich, Zentralbibliothek, Kantons-, Stadt-, und Universitätsbibliothek

CS: Czechoslovakia

Bcsm	Bratislava, Cathedral St. Martin Archiv
Bru	Bratislava, Universitná kniznica
HK	Hradec Králové, Státni vedecká knihovna
OLa	Olomouc, Sátni archív-Arcibiskupská sbírka
Ppp	Prag, Památnik Národního Pisemnictví na Strahove

DDR: East Germany (Deutsche Demokratische Republik)

Bds	Berlin (East), Deutsche Staatsbibliothek
Dl(b)	Dresden, Sächische Landesbibliothek,
GRu	Greifswald, Universitätsbibliothek der ErnstMoritz- Arndt-Universität
Ju	Jena, Universitätsbibliothek der Friedrich Schiller- Universität
Leu	Leipzig, Universitätsbibliothek der Karl-Marx Universität
ROu	Rostock, Universitätsbibliothek
SWl	Schwerin, Wissenschaftliche Allgemeinbibliothek
Z	Zwickau, Ratsschulbibliothek

DK: Denmark

Kk	København, Det kongelige Bibliotek

E: Spain

Bc	Barcelona, Biblioteca Central
Bim	Barcelona, Instituto Español de Musicologia
Boc	Barcelona, Biblioteca Orfeó Catalá
E	Escorial, El, Real Monasterio de El Escorial
GRcr	Granada, Archivo musical de la Capilla Real
Mm	Madrid, Biblioteca municipal
Mmc	Madrid, Biblioteca de la Casa Ducal de Medinaceli
Mp	Madrid, Biblioteca del Palacio real
Sc(o)	Sevilla, Archivo capitular de la Catedral
SE	Segovia, Archivo capitular
SEG	Segorbe, Archivo de la Catedral
V	Valladolid, Archivo musical de la Catedral

F: France

B	Besançon, Bibliothèque municipale
CA	Cambrai, Bibliothèque municipale
Dm	Dijon, Bibliothèque municipale
Nd	Nates, Bibliothèque du Musée Dobrée
Pa	Paris, Bibliothèque de l'Arsenal
Pm	Paris, Bibliothèque Mazarine
Pn	Paris, Bibliothèque nationale
Po	Paris, Bibliothèque-Musée de l'Opéra
Psg	Paris, Bibliothèque Sainte-Geneviève
Pthibault	Paris, Bibliothèque Geneviève Thibault
RO	Roanne, Bibliothèque municipale

GB: Great Britain

Cf	Cambridge, Fitzwilliam Museum
Cmc	Cambridge, Magdalene College
Cu	Cambridge, University Library
Eu	Edinburgh, University Library
Lbm	London, The British Museum/Library
Lcm	London, Royal College of Music
Ll	Lincoln, Cathedral Library
Lu	London, University of London, Music Library
Lwa	London, Westminster Abbey Library
Ob	Oxford, Bodleian Library

Obc	Oxford, Brasenose College
Och	Oxford, Christ Church Library
SH	Sherborne (Dorset), Sherborne School Library
T	Tenbury (Worcestershire), St. Michael's College Library
W	Wells (Somerset), Cathedral Library

H: Hungary

Bn	Budapest, Országos Széchény Könyvtár (Széchényiskt Nationalbibliothek)

I: Italy

Ae	Assisi, Biblioteca comunale
Bc	Bologna, Civieo Museo Bibliografico-Musicale
BGi	Bergamo, Biblioteea civica 'Angelo Maj'
BRd	Brescia, Archivio del Duomo
Bsp	Bologna, Arehivio di San Petronio
CMbc	Casale Monferrato, Biblioteca civica
Fc	Firenze (Florence), Biblioteca del Conservatorio di Musica 'L. Cherubini'
FEc	Ferrara, Biblioteca comunale Ariostea
Fn	Firenze (Florence), Biblioteca Nazionale Centrale
Fol	Foligno, Biblioteca comunale
Fr	Firenze (Florence), Biblioteca Riccardiana
FZc	Faenza, Biblioteca comunale
Ibc	Ivrea Biblioteca capitolare
MC	Monte Cassino, Biblioteca dell'Abbazia
Mcap(d)	Milano, Cappella musicale del Duomo
MOd	Modena, Archivio capitolare
MOe	Modena, Biblioteca Estense
Mt	Milano, Biblioteca Trivulziana e Archivio Storico Civico
Nc	Napoli, Biblioteca del Conservatorio di Musica S. Pietro a Maiella
PAc	Parma, Sezione Musicale della Biblioteca Palatina presso il Conservatorio 'Arrigo Boito'
PAVu	Pavia, Biblioteca universitaria
PCd	Piacenza, Archivio del Duomo
PEc	Perugia, Biblioteca comunale Augusta
PLn	Palermo, Biblioteca nazionale
Pu	Padova, Biblioteca universitaria
Rc	Roma, Biblioteca Casanatense
Rsc	Roma, Biblioteca Musicale governativa del Conservatorio de Santa Cecilia
Rvat	Roma, Biblioteca Apostolica Vaticana

Sd	Siena, Archivio Musicale dell'opera del Duomo
Tn	Torino, Biblioteca nazionale universitaria
TRc	Trent, Biblioteca Comunale
TRmd	Trent, Musco Diocesano
TRmn	Trent, Musco Nazionale .
TVca(d,p)	Treviso, Archivio della Cappella del Duomo
VEcap	Verona, Biblioteca capitolare (Cattedrale)
Vnm	Venezia, Biblioteca nazionale Marciana

Nt: The Netherlands

Avnm	Amsterdam, Bibliotheek der Vereeniging voor Nederlandse Muziekgeschiedenis
DHgm	Den Haag, Gemeente Museum
L	Leiden, Gemeentearchief
Lu	Leiden, Universiteitsbibliotheek
SH	's Hertogenbosch, Archief van de Illustre Lieve Vrouwe Broederschap
Uu	Utrecht, Universiteitsbibliotheek

P: Portugal

Pm	Porto, Biblioteca Pública Municipal

PL: Poland

GD	Gdansk (Danzig), Biblioteka Polskiej Akademii Nauk
Kk	Kraków, Kapitula Metropolitana
KO	Kornik (Kurnik), Biblioteka Polskiej Akademii Nauk
Pr	Poznan (Posen), Archiwum Archidiecezji
Tm	Torun (Thorn), Ksiaznica Miejska im. M. Kopernika
WRu	Wroclaw (Breslau), Biblioteka Uniwersytecka
Wu	Warszawa (Warschau), Biblioteka Uniwersytecka

S: Sweden

Skma	Stockholm, Kungliga Musikaliska Akademiens Bibliotek
Uu	Uppsala, Universitetsbiblioteket
V	Västeras, Stifts- och Landsbiblioteket

US: The United States of America

BLI	Bloomington, Indiana University, Lilly Library
CA	Cambridge (Mass.), Harvard University, Music Libraries
Cn	Chicago, Newberry Library
NH	New Haven (Conn.), Yale University, The Library of the School of Music
NYp	New York, New York Public Library at Lincoln Center
SM	San Marino (Calif.), Henry E. Huntington Library & Art Gallery
U	Urbana (Ill.), University of Illinois, Music Library
Wc	Washington, D.C., Library of Congress, Music Division

USSR: Union of Soviet Socialist Republics

K	Kaliningrad (Königsberg), Oblastnaja biblioteka

Acknowledgments

The reader is indebted for the second edition of this book to Mr. Craig Dabelstein of Brisbane, Australia. Without his contribution to design and all things involved as an editor this book would never again have been available.

David Whitwell
Austin, 2012

PART I
Fourteenth-Century Sources

Fourteenth-Century Sources

ENGLAND

Manuscript Collections Without Instrument Designation

GB:Ob (MS. e Mus. 7), mid-fourteenth century from Bury St Edmunds (Benedictine). Contains 1 textless work in three voices.

GB:Lbm (MS. Harleian 978), contains original dance music in two-voices. Three examples in modern notation can be found in *Archiv für Musik-Wissenschaft* (1918–1919) and three examples are recorded in the 'Archive' series (II, B).

FRANCE

Manuscript Collections Without Instrument Designation

I:Ibc (without shelf-mark), dating 1320–1375, in Avignon, possibly the court of Gaston Fèbus, contains 2 two-part textless works.

F:CA (MS. 29), this manuscript, dating ca. 1381, contains three-part works with text in one voice and text incipits in two and one polyphonic textless fragment.

THE GERMAN-SPEAKING COUNTRIES

Manuscript Collections Without Instrument Designation

BRD:BAa (MS. Ed.IV, 6 fol. 63v), contains an original three-part example of dance music entitled, 'In speculum viellatoris.' A modern edition can be found in *Archiv für Musik-Wissenschaft* (1918–1919).

A:HE (MS. without shelf-mark), ca. 1400, Austria, contains 1 textless composition.

Single Title Manuscripts Designated for Winds

A:Wn (MS. 2856, 'Spörl Liederbuch'), containing 25 sacred and 22 secular works by Hermann, Monk of Salzburg (1350–1410). Three of these compositions are specifically recommended for performance by wind ensembles and one is named for a wind instrument:

Nr. 11. 'Das Nachthorn, vnd is gut zu blasen.'
Nr. 12. 'Das taghorn, auch gut zu blasen, und is sein pum hart dy erst note vnd yr under-octaua slecht him.' This is the earliest known designation of the larger shawm member; the bombard.
Nr. 13. 'Das kchuhorn.'
Nr. 15. 'Das haizt dy trumpet vnd ist auch gut zu blasen.'

These works are in two-parts, but Nr. 15 contains in the upper voice indications of 'Er' and 'Sy' which mean alternating voices, hence a three-part work.

BRD:Nst (MS. Fragment lat. 9, formerly CENT-V, 61), dating from ca. 1390–1410 and containing an anonymous instrumental piece entitled, 'bobik blasen.' Reaney believes this is an example of the kind of wind ensemble literature mentioned by Froissart.[1]

ITALY

Manuscript Collections Without Instrument Designation

I:Fn (MS. Panciatichi 26), dating ca. 1380–1400, contains 1 polyphonic textless composition.

THE LOW COUNTRIES

Manuscript Collections Without Instrument Designation

NL:Lu (MS. 2720), contains Dutch and Flemish works of the Ars Nova style, including a three-part work with only the text incipit 'o,' with the apparent indication of the composer, Sale (fl. ca. 1400).

---

[1] Gilbert Reaney, 'The Performance of Medieval Music' in *Aspects of Medieval and Renaissance Music* (New York: Norton, 1966), 710ff. This article also contains an interesting discussion of medieval percussion music.

PART 2

Fifteenth-Century Sources

Fifteenth-Century Sources

BOHEMIA

Manuscript Collections Without Instrument Designation

CS:BRu (MS. Inc. 318–I), contains 1 polyphonic textless work, ca. 1460.

CS:OLa (MS. c.o.362), contains 1 polyphonic textless fragment, ca. 1470–1480.

CS:Ppp (MS. D.G.IV.47), contains a three-part instrumental work by Johannes Touront (ca. 1450–1480). Additional instrumental examples by Touront can be found in BRD:Mbs (MS. Clm 14274 and MS. 3725) and in the manuscript following.

CS:HK (MS. II.A.7), contains 5 polyphonic textless compositions from late fifteenth and early sixteenth century Prague, including one by Touront.

ENGLAND

Manuscript Collections Without Instrument Designation

GB:Cu (MS. Ff.6.16), contains 1 early fifteenth century polyphonic textless work.

GB:Lbm (MS. Eg.3307), dating from ca. 1430–1444, contains 1 textless carol.

GB:Ob (MS. Lincoln College Latin 89), contains 2 polyphonic textless fragments, ca. early fifteenth century.

GB:Ob (MS. Douce 381), contains 1 instrumental work, ca. 1425.

GB:Ob (MS. Archivum Seldenianum B. 26), contains 1 polyphonic textless work, ca. 1425–1440, probably from Worcester Abbey.

GB:Ob (MS. Ashmole 191), contains 1 polyphonic textless work, ca. 1445–1460.

GB:Cmc (MS. 1236), contains 1 polyphonic textless work, ca. 1460–1465.

GB:W (MS. without shelf-mark), contains 1 polyphonic textless composition, ca. late fifteenth or early sixteenth century.

GB:Lbm (MS. Add. 58445), *Marcha*, by Mario Battagh of Rimini, listed as fifteenth century by the library.

FRANCE AND THE LOW COUNTRIES

Manuscript Collections Without Instrument Designation

F:Pn (MS. Res. 862), contains three-part compositions with text in one voice and text incipits or no text in the remaining voices.

F:Pthibault (MS. Chansonnier Nivelle de la Chaussee), contains three- and four-part works with text in one voice and text incipits in the remaining voices.

I:TRc (MS. 1947/4), a late fifteenth or early sixteenth century manuscript containing 4 polyphonic textless compositions.

US:NH ('Mellon Chansonnier'), contains 57 three-part works with text in the superius and text incipits in the remaining two voices.

E:SEG (Codex), contains three- and four-part works some textless and some with text incipits. Among the textless ones are 10 four-part Dutch instrumental compositions, one of which, Obrecht's 'Ic draghe de mutse clutse,' may be found in a modern edition by Greenberg.[1]

F:Dm (MS. 517), dating ca. 1470–1475 and associated with the Dukes of Burgundy, the manuscript contains 161 compositions, including three-part works with text in one voice and text incipits in the remaining voices; four-part works with text ,in one voice and incipits in the remaining voices; and 1 polyphonic textless work. One example, Busnois's 'Je ne

[1] Noah Greenberg, ed., *An Anthology of Early Renaissance Music* (New York: Norton, 1975).

puis vivre ainsi tousjours,' is contained in Greenberg[2] and twenty-six of these works are contained in a modern edition by Barret.[3]

US:Wc (MS. M.2.1.M.6. Case), a late fifteenth century manuscript containing three-part works with text incipits in all voices.

I:Rvat (Fondo chigiani, MS. C. VIII. 234), dated ca. 1498–1503 and associated with Netherland courts, contains 1 polyphonic textless work.

Pipelare, Matthaeus (ca. 1450–1515). Grove cites a Motet, 'Ave castissima,' with text incipits in all four parts and a chanson, 'Morkin ic hebbe,' with text incipits in all four voices.[4]

[2] Ibid.

[3] Edward Barret, 'The Dijon Chansonnier' (MA Thesis, University of Louisville, 1964).

[4] Grove, 14:765. Modern editions of these works are cited in the composer's complete works in 'CMM xxxiv/1–3; i, 9 and 9, 4 respectively.'

THE GERMAN-SPEAKING COUNTRIES

Manuscript Collections Without Instrument Designation

BRD:W (MS. Guelferbytanus 30.9.2. Augusteus 40), contains 1 polyphonic textless work from the early fifteenth century.

BRD:Mbs (MS. Clm 14274, formerly Mus. Ms. 3232a), dated ca. 1430–1450, from the Benedictine cloister of St. Emmeram in Regensburg contains works from the last decade of the fourteenth century to mid-fifteenth century including 21 textless compositions and three-part works with text in one voice and textless in the remaining two.

BRD:Mbs (MS. 3224), a collection of early fifteenth century fragments, containing 1 textless work.

A:Wn (MS. 5094), dated ca. 1420–1450, perhaps Nürnberg, contains 2 polyphonic textless works.

BRD:W (MS. Guelferbytanus 892 Helmstadiensis), dated 1451, Hildesheim, contains 2 polyphonic textless works.

BRD:B (MS. 40613, 'Lochamer Liederbuch,' (formerly known as the 'Alteres Nürnberger Liederbuch'), containing works written various hands in Nürnberg, ca. 1455–1460. A major source of German fifteenth-century ensemble music, the manuscript contains 47 anonymous compositions, of which

7 are three-voice, 2 are two-voice, and the rest monophonic. A facsimile edition was made in 1925 by K. Ameln and the 'Archive' series of recordings contains examples under Series III, B.

BRD:As (MS. 142a), dated 1458, includes three-part textless compositions.

BRD:Mbs (MS. Germanicus monocensis 810, 'Schedelsches Liederbuch'), ca. 1460–1470, contains 128 compositions of which 15 are polyphonic textless works and 2 monophonic textless works. This manuscript was compiled by Hartmann Schedel (d. 1514) and acquired in 1552 by John Jacob Fugger and sold to Albrecht v, Duke of Bavaria, in 1571.

DK:Kk (MS. 291/8), ca. 1470–1480, contains three-part works with text in one voice and text incipits or textless in the remaining voices and four-part works with text in one voice and text incipits in the remaining voices. Examples in modern prints can be found in *Revue de Mus.* (VIII), 1927, 12–35.

BRD:B (MS. 40098 'Glogauer Liederbuch'), lost during the last war, this manuscript, dated ca. 1480, contained 59 polyphonic textless works in three and four-parts. This is one of the earliest examples of music appearing in separate part-books for instrumental performance. Four of these works are recorded on the 'Archive' series (III, B) and one, an anonymous, 'Die Katzn Pföte' ('the cat's paw') appears in a modern edition in Greenberg.[5]

BRD:B (MS. 40021), ca. 1495, contains 18 polyphonic works without text.

DDR:LEu (MS. 1494), late fifteenth century choirbook containing 21 polyphonic textless works including a three-part setting of 'La Spagna.' This manuscript is perhaps an example of university music as it can be associated with the university from 1492–1537.

PL:Wu (MS. Rps.Mus.58), dating ca. 1500 from the Silesian-Bohemian border, contains 2 textless compositions, one of which is a three-part setting of 'La Spagna.'

[5] Greenberg, *An Anthology of Early Renaissance Music.*

BRD:W (MS. 287), ca. 1480–1490, contains three-part works with text in one voice and text incipits in the remaining two voices.

PL:Wu (MS. Mf 2016), ca. 1500, contains 11 textless compositions.

DDR:LEu (cited in Grove, 6:561), 5 textless compositions (1494) by Heinrich Finck (1444–1527).

Works Associated with Maximilian I

A:Wn (MS. 18810), ca. 1524, contains three and four-part instrumental compositions with text incipits in all voices, including works by Isaac ('Carmen in fa') and Antoine Brumel ('Tandernac').

BRD:Mbs (MS. 328–331), contains three-part dance music by Isaac (including, 'Carmen in fa') and a textless version (incomplete) of 'Innsbruck, ich muss dich lassen.'

BRD:Mbs (MS. 3154), ca. 1466–1511, contains 20 textless compositions associated with the imperial court in Innsbruck.

BRD:Mbs (MS. 3155), ca. 1515–1524, contains 3 German secular works without text associated with Maximilian I.

CH:Bu (MS. F .X. 22–24), early sixteenth century, contains four-part compositions with text incipits in all voices (missing the tenor part), containing some instrumental works associated with the imperial court.

CH:SGs (MS.Codex 461), ca. 1545, contains three and four-part anonymous textless works, including some associated with the court of Maximilian I.

BRD:Rp (MS. D. XII), contains a four-part instrumental work by Isaac ('An buos').

I:Fn (MS. Panciatichi 27), contains Isaac's 'A la bataglia.' According to Kämper, fol. 116v in this manuscript is a four-part textless example of a fifteenth-century 'passamezzo antico.'[6]

I:Fn (MS. XIX, 11. 178), contains Isaac's 'J'ay pris amours.'

[6] Dietrich Kämper, *Studien zur Instrumentalen Ensemblemusik des 16. Jahrhunderts in Italien* (Köln, 1970), 46.

ITALY

Manuscript Collections Without Instrument Designation

I:Fr (MS. 2794), a fifteenth-century manuscript, contains three-part works with text in one voice and textless in the remaining two voices and works with only text incipits in all voices.

US:Wc (MS. M2.1.L25 Case, 'Laborde Chansonnier'), contains 106 three-part chansons mostly with text in the superius, a text incipit in the tenor and textless in the contratenor; one work with an Italian incipit in the upper voices with no further text; and one textless French secular work, dating ca. 1475–1485.

F:Pn (MS. 2973, 'Le Chansonnier Cordiforme'), a fifteenth-century manuscript containing three-part works with text in one voice and text incipits in the remaining two.

I:PEc (MS. 431), a fifteenth-century manuscript containing three-part compositions with text in one voice and either text incipits or textless in the remaining two voices; works with incipits in all three voices.

I:Rvat (MS. SP B 80), a fifteenth-century manuscript containing three-part works with text in one voice and text incipits in the remaining two.

I:Pu (MS. 675), early fifteenth century, contains 1 polyphonic textless fragment.

F:Pn (MS. 568), ca. 1405–1408, probably Florence, contains 201 works, some with text incipits only.

I:Rvat (MS. Codex Urbino lat. 1411), contains three-part works with text in one voice and incipits in two voices.

F:Pn (MS. 26,), contains (Nr. 35) a three-part instrumental rondeau by a composer named Marcus, writing in Florence after 1400.

I:FZc (MS. 117), ca. 1410–1420, Northern Italy, contains 1 textless fugue, but as the first portion of the manuscript contains keyboard music (although in a different hand) the suggestion has been made that this fugue may also have been intended for keyboard.

GB:Lbm (MS. Cotton Titus, A. XXVI), ca. 1420–1449, Northern Italy, perhaps Venice, contains some French secular works which are textless.

I:Bu (MS. 2216), contains a motet, 'O Thoma Didime,' by Do. Vala (fl. 1430–1440) which has a prelude and postlude which Grove (19:488) suggests may be instrumental.

I:MC (MS. 871), ca. 1430–1480, contains 141 works including 5 three- and four-part textless compositions; four-part works with text incipits in all voices; and nearly all remaining works have full text only in the upper voice.

I:Vnm (MS. 7554), ca. 1430–1440, from a Franciscan establishment in Venice, contains 2 textless works.

I:Bc (MS. Q 15), ca. 1440, contains three-part works with text in one voice and textless in the remaining voices. The manuscript contains a work by Matheus de Brixia (fl. 1412-1419, Vicenza), 'Jesu postquam monstraverat,' which has an instrumental prelude in four-parts.

I:TRmn (MS. 92), ca. 1440, contains three-part works with text in one voice and either text incipits or textless in the remaining voices.

I:MOe (MS. a.X.I,ii), ca. 1450, contains three-part works with text in one voice and text incipits in the remaining two.

I:PAVu (MS. Aldini 361), mid-fifteenth century, contains 2 polyphonic textless works.

I:TRmn (MS. 92), contains a four-voice textless work by Andreas Tallafangi Calabr (fl. 1440–1450).

I:Fn (MS. Magl. XIX, 112bis), dates from the Genoese ducal palace, ca. 1456, contains three-part works with text in one voice and either textless or with text incipits in the remaining two voices and one work which is entirely textless.

I:TRmd (MS. 93), ca. 1460, contains three-part works with text incipits in two voices and textless in the third.

I:TRmn (MS. 90), ca. 1460, contains three-part compositions with text in one voice and either textless or with text incipits in the remaining two.

I:PAVu (MS. Aldini 362), ca. late 1460s or early 1470s, probably from Savoy, contains three-part compositions with text only in the upper voice and either incipits or textless in the remaining two voices and 1 polyphonic textless composition.

E:E (MS. IV.a.24), ca. 1460–1470, Naples, contains 118 three-part chansons with text in one voice and either text incipits or no text in the remaining two voices and 3 polyphonic textless compositions.

BRD:B (MS. 78.C.28, formerly Hamilton 451), ca. 1465, contains 41 anonymous polyphonic textless works (concordances prove most to be French chansons) and 1 secular composition with text added in a later hand. The manuscript was copied in Naples as a wedding gift for the Florentine couple, Margherita Castellani and Bernardino Niccolini.

I:TRmn (MS. 89), ca. 1470, contains three-part works with text in one voice and text incipits in the remaining two and works which are entirely textless.

I:PAc (MS. 1158), ca. 1472–1474, contains 4 polyphonic textless works.

I:Fn (MS. Magliabeachi XIX. 176), ca. 1470s, Florence, contains 4 polyphonic textless compositions as well as works with text in only one voice.

I:Bu (MS. 2573), ca. 1475, Bologna, contains 4 polyphonic textless compositions.

E:Sc(o) (MS. 5-1-43), ca. 1470–1485, probably Naples, contains 123 three and four-part compositions, including 1 textless Italian secular work; 3 textless French secular works; 4 polyphonic textless compositions; and works with text only in the superius and text incipits in the remaining voices. This is a divided manuscript, with 38 works originally found here now contained in F:Pn (MS. 4379), together with another 6 works divided between the two manuscripts. In F:Pn (MS. 4379) there is an additional polyphonic textless work.

F:Pn (MS. fonds fr. 15123, 'Pixérécourt MS.'), dating ca. 1480, contains 169 three-part works with text in one voice and text incipits in the remaining two; some entirely with incipits; some with text in one voice and textless in the remaining two; four-part works with text in one voice and incipits in the remaining three; and 1 work entirely textless.

I:Fr (MS. 2356), ca. 1480–1485, Florence, contains three-part works with incipits in two voices and textless in the third; three-part works with incipits in all voices; four-part works with an incipit in one voice and textless in the remaining three voices; and 3 polyphonic textless compositions.

I:PEc (MS. 431 [G.20]), ca. 1480–1490, Naples, contains 1 textless hymn; 1 textless Italian secular work; 1 textless French secular work; and 10 other textless works, including a setting of 'La Spagna.'

I:Mcap(d) (MS. Librone 1), ca. 1484–1490, for the Milan Cathedral, contains 2 polyphonic textless compositions.

I:Rc (MS. 2856), ca. 1485–1490, Ferrara, prepared as a wedding gift to Isabella d'Este. According to the *Census Catalogue of Manuscript Sources of Polyphonic Music* (University of Illinois), this manuscript contains 3 textless French secular works, 1 textless Italian secular work, and 3 other textless works. According to Grove, the manuscript contains 123 'wordless compositions.'

I:Bc (MS. Q. 16), Naples, 1487, contains 131 compositions without text.

I:Fol (MS. without shelf-mark), ca. late fifteenth century, Northern Italy, contains 1 polyphonic textless composition.

I:Fn (MS. Banco Rari 229), 1492–1493, Florence, contains 86 textless compositions and most of the remaining 182 have titles or text incipits only.

I:Bc (MS. Q. 17), ca. 1490s, Florence, according to Grove contains 71 compositions almost entirely wordless.

I:Rvat (MS. C.G. XIII 27), Florence, ca. 1492–1494, perhaps for Giuliano de' Medici, contains 108 wordless compositions in three and four parts.

I:Fn (MS. Magl. XIX. 178), Florence, ca. 1490s, contains 74 compositions without text.

I:Bc (MS. Q. 18), 'Northern Italy,' ca. 1500, associated with the Bologna Civic Wind Band, contains 73 compositions without text in three and four parts.

I:Fn (MS. Magliabeachi XIX. 121), ca. 1500, Florence, contains 4 polyphonic textless compositions.

GB:Ob (MS. Canonici Miscellaneous 42), late fifteenth century, Northern Italy, contains 1 polyphonic textless composition.

I:MOe (MS. F.9.9.), 1495–1496, contains 3 polyphonic textless compositions.

I:Rvat (MS. Codicetto Vat.lat.11953), ca. 1500, a surviving bass-part book, corresponding with other known four-part instrumental works.

Print Collections Without Instrument Designation

Odhecaton [Canti A] (Ottaviano Petrucci, Venice, 1501). Copies in I:Bc (imperfect), E:Mmc (1504 edition), F:Pn (1504 edition), I:TVca(d) (1504 edition), and US:Wc.

This is the earliest printed collection of part-music for instrumental performance. Reese[7] believed Petrucci's intent was to present 'raw material' from which copies for specific performances could be drawn. Perhaps it is more to the point to suggest that the printer, Petrucci, was expecting to make sales to the numerous wind bands in Europe who need repertoire. The title, a mixture of Greek and Latin, means, 'One hundred songs of harmonic music,' but the volume actually contains 96 works, of which 49 are three-part and 47 four-part. The music represents the major French and Flemish composers, ca. 1470–1500. Most

[7] Gustave Reese, 'The First Printed Collection of Part-Music,' *The Musical Quarterly* (1934), 155.

of the repertoire is vocal, presented here in an instrumental form, however at least four of the compositions are almost certainly originally conceived for instruments: 'Dit le burguygnon' (fol. 20); 'La morra' (fol. 49), by 'Yzac' (Isaac?); 'La strangetta' (fol. 54), by 'Werbach' (Obrecht?); and 'La alfonsiana' (fol. 87), by Jo. Ghiselin. Works from this collection by Agricola and Compere are available in modern editions by Greenberg[8] and a complete modern edition was made in 1942 by H. Hewitt. A facsimile edition was made in 1932 and a more recent one in 1973 by Brode Brothers.

[8] Greenberg, *An Anthology of Early Renaissance Music*.

Odhecaton [Canti B] (Petrucci, Venice, 1502). Copies in I:Bc and F:Pn.

Canti B contains 50 textless three- and four-part compositions, representing an international sampling of composers, ca. 1470–1500. A modern edition was made by H. Hewitt (Chicago: University of Chicago, 1967).

Odhecaton [Canti C] (Petrucci, Venice, 1504). Copies in F:Pn, A:Wn, and I:TVca(d) (imperfect).

Canti C contains 137 three- and four-part textless compositions, ca. 1470-1500. Josquin's wind band fanfare, 'Vive le roy!,' is contained in this collection and available in a modern edition by Greenberg.[9]

[9] Ibid

Motetti A. (Petrucci, Venice, 1502) Copy in I:Bc.

This volume contains a number of vocal compositions, Latin text. However, two are textless, with text incipits only, and one is a composition for instruments, 'La spagna,' by Ghiselin, in four parts.

POLAND

Manuscript Collections Without Instrument Designation

PL:Wu (MS. 378 Lat. Q) early fifteenth century, Polish, contains 1 textless polyphonic composition.

PL:KO (MS. 801), ca. 1452–1488, contains 2 three-voice textless compositions.

PL:Pr (MS. 1361), late fifteenth century, Poznan Province, contains 1 textless fragment.

SPAIN AND PORTUGAL

Manuscript Collections Without Instrument Designation

E:SE (MS. without shelf-mark), fifteenth century, contains three-part compositions with an incipit in one voice and textless in the remaining two voices.

P:Pm (MS. 714), ca. 1450, contains three-part compositions with text in one voice and either text incipits or no text in the remaining two voices.

E:Sc(o) (MS.7-I-28), ca. 1490s, contains three-part works with text in one voice and text incipits in the remaining voices; four-part works with text in one voice and either incipits or no text in the remaining voices; and four-part works with incipits in all voices.

E:Bc (MS. 454), Spanish, late fifteenth century, contains 10 textless compositions.

MUSIC OF THE BASSE-DANCE

In no other area of fifteenth-century music is there so wide a divergence between the actual surviving music and the known practice of the time. Although both the fact that the basse-dance was performed primarily by the wind band and the wide spread extent of this practice has been long known, very little music is preserved. The reason for this lies in the performance practice in which only the melody was consistent and the other two or three voices were improvised. Thus most surviving sources give only the melody, as found in the 'tenor.'

B:Bc (MS. 9085), contains 52 basse-dance melodies, together with the dance instruction associated with them. The material is almost identical with that in a published volume (before 1496), *Le Art et instruction de bien dancer* by Toulouze.

The Toulouze publication contains five tenors which are not in the Brussels manuscript; both are probably based on a common, earlier source which is now unknown.

GB:Lbm (MS. Add. 29987), contains at least 15 dance tenors, all of which are found in a modern edition in *Archive für Musik-Wissenschaft* (1918–1919). Four examples are recorded in the 'Archive' series (II, B).

F:Pn (MS. fr. 844, 'Chanssonnier du roi '). Three dance tenors from this manuscript are recorded in the 'Archive' series (II, B).

I:Rvat (MS. 1725, and MS. 1490). One dance tenor from each manuscript is included in the 'Archive' recording series (II, B).

I:TRmn (Codex MS. 87), first-half, fifteenth century contains (in Nrs. 83, 90, and 160) a three-part arrangement of a basse-dance tenor.

GB:Ob (MS. Digby 167), contains 2 basse-dance tenors, ca. 1450–1475.

I:Bc (MS. 109, fol. 59v–60), contains an imperfect copy of a polyphonic dance composition, entitled, 'La bassa Castaglya.'

E:Mp (MS. 2-1-5, f. 223), contains a three-part setting of the same tune found above, here called, 'La Spagna.' In this version the middle voice is marked, 'Alta,' leading Besseler to conclude the entire work is for wind band.[10] A modern edition of this version can be found in Davison-Apel, *Harvard Anthology*, Nr. 102a.

I:PEc (MS. 431, fol. 95v–96), contains a late fifteenth-century setting of the same tune, corresponding with the imperfect version in I:Bc (MS. 109).

[10] Friedrich Blume, ed., *Die Musik in Geschichte und Gegenwart* (Kassel: Bärenreiter, 1949–1968), under 'Alta.'

PART 3
Sixteenth-Century Sources

Sixteenth-Century Sources

AUSTRIA

Manuscript Collections Without Instrument Designation

Several Austrian manuscripts of the sixteenth century have fifteenth-century material as well and are given above in Part 2 under, 'Works Associated with Maximilian I.'

Single Title Prints Designated for Any Instrument

Hofhaimer (Hofheimer), Paul, 1459–1537

Harmoniae poeticae ... tum vocibus humanis, tum etiam instrumentis accommodatissimae. (Nürnberg, Johann Petreius, 1539, four parts). Copies in A:Wn, BRD:B, F:Pn, GB:Lbm, I:Rc, I:Vnm, and US:Wc.

BOHEMIA

Manuscript Collections Without Instrument Designation

CS:HK (MS. II.A.20), early sixteenth century, contains 9 textless polyphonic works.

CS:HK (MS. II.A.29), ca. 1556–1562, contains 2 textless polyphonic compositions.

CS:Bcsm (MS. 11), 1571, Bratislava, contains 1 polyphonic composition.

DENMARK

Manuscript Collections Without Instrument Designation

DK:Kk (MS. Gamle Kongelige Samling 1872), ca. 1550, Repertoire of the Danish Royal instrumentalists.

DK:Kk (MS. Gamle Kongelige Samling 1873/4), ca. 1556, five part-books, containing 133 works with titles or text incipits only and 29 works entirely textless. This manuscript is associated with the Danish court of King Christian III, 1534–1559, and probably represents part of his wind band repertoire.

DK:Kk (MS. R141), ca. 1556, an anonymous collection of 25 instrumental dances in five part-books.

DK:Kk (MS. Thott 1848), ca. 1525, contains three- and four-part works with text in one voice only.

Single Title Manuscripts Without Instrument Designation

1556 Group of Single Titles

The following manuscripts are all dated ca. 1556, associated with the court of Christian III, consisting of four or five parts, always with one part missing. A few parts carry an instrument designation, always a wind instrument. Composers who have been identified but whose name does not appear in the part-books are given in parenthesis. Compositions carry either text incipits or titles, as given. The DK:Kk catalog number is given in parenthesis.

Anonymous, [No Title] (R134)
Anonymous, [No Title] (R137)
Anonymous, [No Title] (R138)
Anonymous, [No Title] (R139)
Anonymous, [No Title] (R136)
Anonymous, [No Title] (R140)
Anonymous, [No Title] (R74)
Anonymous, *Au despartir* (R58)
Anonymous, *Constitues Eos* (R98)
Anonymous, *Der Tag der ist so freudenreich* (R116)
Anonymous, *Ecce Dominus veniet* (R90)
Anonymous, *Engelbocgen dantz* (R142)
Anonymous, *En quam honesta* (R45)
Anonymous, *Gelobet seyst du Jesu Christ* (R118)
Anonymous, *Hellas dama* (R54)
Anonymous, *Mentre per questi* (R113)
Anonymous, *Mich wundert gar hardt* (R122)

Anonymous, *Parcere prostrates* (R123)
Anonymous, *Propter peccata* (R33)
Anonymous, *Quem nos merito* (R76, one part is called, 'Krumhorn')
Anonymous, *Sancta Maria* (R84, one part is called, 'Krumhorn')
Anonymous, *Se pur ti guardi* (R135, one part is marked, 'Auff Zinken')
Anonymous, *Se pur ti guardo* (R112)
Anonymous, *Su, su, su ... a la battaglia* (R130)
Anonymous, *Vater unser* (R37)
Anonymous, *Vous qui* (R111)
Anonymous, *Wer ich ein falck* (R124)
Anonymous, *Zu Gott mein Trost allein*, one part gives, *Sonst anders kein Heiland* (R106)
[Abell, Dav.], *In dulce jubilo* (R117)
[Amsfortius, Franciscus], *Christ ist erstanden* (R104)
[Arcadelt, Jacques, 1507–1668], *Recordare Domine* (R69)
[Baston, Josquin, 1515–1576], *Dum transisset sabbatum* (R39)
[Baston, Josquin], *Le bon espoir* (R1)
[Baston, Josquin], *Vostre a jamais* (R10)
[Berchem, Jacob van, 1505–1567], *Surge petre* (R79)
[Braetel, Huldrich, 1495–1544], *So ich betracht* (R49)
[Briant, Denis], *Quant me souient* (R63)
[Bultel, Jacob], *Homo quidam fecit* (R93)
[Canis, Cornelius, 1510–1561], *Belle donne moy* (R11)
Canis, Cornelius, *Domine quis habitabit* (R80)
[Canis, Cornelius], *Pour parvenir* (R16)
[Castileti, Johannes, 1512–1588] *Tant seulement ton amour* (R133)
[Chastelain, Joannes], *Je ne desire que la mort* (R13)
[Clemens non Papa, 1510–1566] *A qui me doit* (R86)
[Clemens non Papa], *Amour au Coeur* (R127)
[Clemens non Papa], *Ave martir gloriosa* (R57)
[Clemens non Papa], *Aymer estma vie* (R27)
[Clemens non Papa], *Clemens et benigna* (R85)
Clemens non Papa, *Ego flos campi* (R120)
[Clemens non Papa], *Fremuit spiritus Jesu* (R94)
Clemens non Papa, *Hic est vere martyr* (R99)
Clemens non Papa, *Ite in orbem* (R40)
[Clemens non Papa], *L'aultrier me* (R7)
Clemens non Papa, *La non ailliers* (R30)

Clemens non Papa, *Leuavi oculos meos* (R97)
[Clemens non Papa], *Maria Magdalena et altera maria* (R41)
[Clemens non Papa], *Me retirer* (R56)
[Clemens non Papa], *Misit me vivens* (R35)
Clemens non Papa, *O Maria* (R81)
[Clemens non Papa], *Pastores quidnam videistis* (R19)
[Clemens non Papa], *Pater peccavi* (R129)
[Clemens non Papa], *Si par souffrir* (R51)
[Clemens non Papa], *Virgo prudentissima* (R100)
[Cocq, Gerard de], *Ung cuer en devil je porte* (R4)
[Courtois, Jean], *Tout jour Le al* (R107)
[Crequillon, Thomas, 1505–1557], *Adiuva nos dues* (R3)
Crecquillon, *Congregati sunt* (R78)
[Crecquillon], *Deus virtutum* (R2)
[CrecquilIon], *Dictes pourquoy* (R12)
[CrecquilIon], *Dieu me fault* (R6)
Crecquillon, *Domine da nobis* (R65)
[Crecquillon], *J'ai veu sans* (R5)
[Crecquillon], *Je changerai* (R9)
Crecquillon, *Je changerai quelque chose* (R28)
[Crecquillon], *O triste ennuye* (R15)
[Crecquillon], *Or puisqu'envi* (R20)
[Crecquillon], *Pardonnez moy* (R14)
Crecquillon, *Si me tenes tant de riguer* (R75)
[Crespel, Joannes (Jean), 16th c. French], *A la devenir toujours* (R17)
[Crespel], *Chant musical* (R8)
[Crespel], *Dame d'honneur* (R21)
[Crespel], *Jay veu le cerfz* (R55)
Crespel, *Le content est riche en ce monde* (R71)
[Crespel], *Sourtoute fleur j'aime* (R18)
[De Latre, Claude Petit. d/ 1598], *Si seule estois* (R89)
[Despres (des Prez), Josquin, 1450–1521, French], *Faute d'argent* (R23)
[Despres, Josquin], *Haeac dicit dominis* (R46)
Despres, Josquin, *In illo tempore* (R91)
[Despres, Josquin], *Messe point* (R59)
[Despres, Josquin], *Petite Camusette* (R62)
[Despres, Josquin], *Pour souhaiter* (R61)
[Despres, Josquin], *Stabat mater dolorosa* (R31)
[Despres, Josquin], [*Tulerunt Dominum*], [No text] (R131)

[Ducis, Benedictus, 1492–1544, German], *Ave maris stella* (R101)

Eckel, Mathias, d. 1538, *Ecce nunc benedicite* (R68)

[Festa, Constantio, 1490–1545, Franco-Flemish composer], *Hierusalem quae occidis* (R42)

[Fevin, Antonius, 1470–1512, Franco-Flemish], *Santa trinitas* (R114)

Gombert, Nicolas, 1495–1560, *Oculi omnium* (R77)

Gombert, N., *Peccata mea sicut* (R66)

[Hellinck (also Lupi, Lupus), Joannes], *In te domine speravi* (R32)

[Hollandre], *Celle quima fant* (R53)

Hollandre, *Forte fortune fors* (R70)

[Hollandre], *Je L'ay aime* (R26)

[Jannequin, Clement, 1485–1558], *Die Schlacht Paffia* (R43)

[Larchier, Joannes], *D'amour me plais* (R50)

Larchier, Joannes, *Nisi quia Dominus erat* (R96)

[Lasso, Orlando, 1530–1594], *Congratulamini* (R109)

[Lasso, Orlando], *Qua re tristis est anima mea* (R110)

Lupi, Jean, *Pastores Loquebantur* (R29)

[Manchicourt, Pierre], *Illuminare Jerusalem* (R82)

[Manchicourt], *Qui est ista qui ascendit* (R88)

[Manchicourt], *Sustinuimus pacem* (R92)

[Manchicourt], *Tota pulchra es amica mea* (R95)

[Milan, Cornet de], *Le departir* (R22)

[Mouton, Jean], *Tua est potential* (R24)

Paston, Johan, *Christ ist erstanden* (R105)

(Phinot, Domenico), *Jam non dicam* (R128)

[Rore, Cipriano de], *Mon petit* (R126)

[Senfl, Ludwig], *Ach Meidlein rein wer ich allein* (R44)

[Senfl], *De profundis* (R34)

[Senfl], *Philippe qui videt me* (R102)

[Senfl], *Was wirt es doch* (R121)

Stoltzer, Thomas, *Nesciens mater* (R125)

Tubal, A., *Tous Les plaisirs* (R73)

Vinders, Hieronymus, *Omors inevitabilis* (R119)

[Waelrant, Hubert], *Mais Languirai-je* (R52)

[Waelrant], *Verba mea auribus* (R83, one part is marked, 'Krumhorn.')

[Walter, Johann?], *Nun bitten wir den heilgen Geist* (R36)

[Walter?], *Verbum domini* (R47)

[Walter?], *Wir glauben all an einem Gott* (R48)
[Wannenmcher, Johann], *Du schnoede Tochter Babylon* (R115)
[Willaert, Adrian], *Creator omnium deus terribilis* (R60)
[Willaert], *Fors seulement* (R64)
[Wismes, Nicholas de], *Je nay quelque* (R103)
[Wismes], *Qui est ista qui processit* (R87)

1580 Group of Single Titles

The following manuscripts are all dated ca. 1580 and associated with the court of Frederik II (1559–1588). All consist of only one part, the remaining parts are missing. Given is the incipit each carries and in parenthesis the DK:Kk catalog number.

Anonymous, *Da Le piu* (R648)
Anonymous, *Dech co-si* (R640)
Anonymous, *Deh non Mo-strat* (R647)
Anonymous, *Dianam, Rectius, Lydia, Non, Solvitur* (R448)
Anonymous, *Got wolt* (R658)
Anonymous, *In questo* (R653)
Anonymous, *Las-so gia* (R645)
Anonymous, *Laura soave* (R639)
Anonymous, *Lova La nott* (R650)
Anonymous, *Mir gleibt in grumme* (R398)
Anonymous, *Movi cor mio* (R656)
Anonymous, *O bella mano* (R642)
Anonymous, *Ogni mia speme* (R654)
Anonymous, *Quand uscir* (R644)
Anonymous, *Quando nei bel* (R651)
Anonymous, *Se quant* (R649)
Anonymous, *Si vox est canta* (R338)
Anonymous, *State Longi da me* (R657)
Anonymous, *Valli vicine e rupi* (R652)

1582 Group of Single Titles

The following manuscripts are all dated ca. 1582 and associated with the court of Frederik II. All consist of two part-books; two part-books are missing. Given are the original text incipits and in parenthesis the DK:Kk catalog number.

Anonymous, [No Title or text] (R202)
Anonymous, [No text] (R197)

Anonymous, [No text] (R196)
Anonymous, [No text] (R195)
Anonymous, *Elle craint* (R194)
Anonymous, *Ia mi trovai* (R199)
Anonymous, *Io mi son giove nell* (R198)
Anonymous, *Madonna* (R212)
Anonymous, *Le Rossignol* (R208)
Anonymous, *O Le grand bien* (R207)
Anonymous, *O sogno mio felice* (R209)
Anonymous, *O tant vous* (R203)
Anonymous, *Peter Reny* (R204)
Anonymous, *Quand je me trouve* (R205)
Anonymous, *Rosenobe* (R206)
Anonymous, *Sortez, regrez* (R210)
Anonymous, *Soupirs* (R201)

1588 Group of Single Titles

The following manuscripts are all dated ca. 1588 and associated with the court of either Frederik II or Christian IV, 1588–1648. All consist of two part-books; two or three part-books are missing. Given are the original text incipits and in parenthesis the DK:Kk catalog number.

Anonymous, *Deh ferm amor* (R245)
Anonymous, *Deh perche ciel* (R260)
Anonymous, *Ecce quam bonum* (R274)
Anonymous, *Ecce venit tibi* (R273)
Anonymous, *En d'ou viennes vous* (R282)
Anonymous, *Et re-spon-dens Je-sus* (R270)
Anonymous, *Medtlein* (R268)
Anonymous, *Ogni Logo mi porge* (R280)
Anonymous, *Omnes sitientes venite* (R271)
Anonymous, *Pass e Mezo* (R285)
Anonymous, *Poi che per ben* (R252)
Anonymous, *Puon fin* (R267)
Anonymous, *Sa quest altier* (R244)
Anonymous, *Sorgi* (R281)
Anonymous, *Saltarello* (R278)
Anonymous, *Veni ditelo mi* (R275)
Anonymous, *Vina parant animos* (R276)
Alessandrino, Venetiano, *Sia vil a gl'altri* (R259)

Anselmo, *S'altri s'afflig' et duo* (R254)
Arcadelt, Jacob, *Laer gravato* (R247)
Barre, Antonio, *Dunque fiave* (R243)
Barre, Antonio, *Non e pena maggior* (R250)
Dankers, Ghiselin, *Fedel qual sempre* (R249)
Domenico, Joan, *Posto ch'il sol* (R258)
Ferro, Vincenzo, *Carro di tanti* (R248)
Lamberto, *Oime, Oime* (R255)
Lasso, O., *Di pensier* (R284)
Lasso, O., *Las ie n'ira plus* (R277)
Lupacchino, Bernardino, *Il dolce sonno* (R257)
Lupacchino, B., *Occhi leggiatri* (R256)
Sezza, Gratiano Fido di, *Apollo volch' i moia* (R221)
Sezza, G.F. di, *Cofumando mi* (R217)
Sezza, G.F., *Da hora* (R224)
Sezza, G., *Deh Lor fosa io* (R219)
Sezza, G., *Diti in tj* (R215)
Sezza, G., *I non hebbj* (R216)
Sezza, G., *Lasso che mela i costo* (R223)
Sezza, G., *Le sitta son* (R218)
Sezza, G., *Mont hatant* (R214)
Sezza, G., *Qual clina* (R225)
Sezza, G., *Sel dissi maj* (R222)
Sezzi, G., *Sopra dur* (R220)
Sezzi, G., *Spiegato hora* (R213)
Sezza, Paolo Gigli di, *A i rudo* (R230)
Sezza, P., *A questo* (R232)
Sezza, P., *[Canzon]* (No text) (R231)
Sezza, P., *Cato dulc' alto* (R228)
Sezza, P., *Chi e fermono* (R234)
Sezzo, P., *Chiuso gran* (R236)
Sezza, P., *Come Lune di notte* (R237)
Sezza, P., *Di Suit* (R233)
Sezza, P., *Lasso merch' i non* (R240)
Sezza, P., *Laura soa* (R235)
Sezza, P., *Misero romi mai* (R227)
Sezza, P., *Non perch' io sia* (R238)
Sezza, P., *Quando volte* (R229)
Sezza, P., *Sio essi vino* (R239)
Sezza, P., *Sporgo tra i gigli* (R226)
Sezza, P., *Un Lauro* (R241)
Tostolo, Giulian, *Miser in van* (R253)

ENGLAND

Manuscript Collections Without Instrument Designation

GB:Ob (MS. Digby 133), ca. 1505, contains 1 polyphonic textless composition.

GB:Lbm (MS. Royal 20.A.XVI), sixteenth century, contains three-part works with text in the superius and incipits in the remaining two voices.

GB:Lbm (MS. Add. 31922, 'Henry VIII'), ca. 1510–1520, contains 35 polyphonic textless three- and four-part compositions and a number of others with only titles or incipits. The manuscript includes the textless three-part, 'Fortuna desperata,' by Busnois and the 'alles regretz,' of Ghizeghim, with text in the tenor.

GB:Lbm (MS. Royal Appendix 74–76), ca. 1547–1548, contains 40 polyphonic textless works, including canons and dances. One of the original four part-books is missing.

GB:Ob (MS. Music School e. 420–422), ca. 1549–1552, London, three part-books, contains 1 textless work.

GB:Lbm (MS. Harley 7578), second-half, sixteenth century, contains 4 polyphonic textless works.

GB:Lbm (MS. Add. 30480–30484), ca. 1560–1590, five part-books, contains 4 textless works.

GB:Eu (MS. La.III.483), compiled by Thomas Wode, 1562 to ca. 1590, three part-books, contains 3 four-part dances, a three-part instrumental work by Cowper, and 2 'In Nomines' by Tallis, in four-parts. GB:Lbm (MS. Add. 33933), an imperfect copy, also contains an 'Air.'

GB:Lbm (MS. Add. 22597), ca. 1565–1585, only one of five original part-books, contains 16 textless compositions.

GB:Ob (MS. Tenbury 1464), ca. 1570–1575, only one of the original part-books, contains 11 instrumental works.

GB:Ob (MS. Music School e. 423), ca. 1575–1586, only one surviving part-book, contains 11 instrumental works.

GB: Lbm (MS. Add. 31390, 'A booke of In nomines & other solfainge songes of v: vj: vij: & viij pts for voyces or Instrumentes,' 1578 or before, contains 65 instrumental works.

GB:Och (MS. 979–983), ca. 1578–1581, Windsor, five of original six part-books (tenor is missing), contains 6 instrumental works.

GB:Lbm (MS. Add. 47844), ca. 1581, one of original set of part-books, contains three five- and six-part instrumental works by Parsons, Strogers, and Tye. The fly-leaves contain additional textless fragments.

GB:Och (MS. 984–988), ca. 1581–1588, five part-books, contains 13 instrumental works.

GB:Lbm (MS. Add. 32377), ca. 1585–1590, one of original five part-books, contains 35 textless compositions.

US:NH (MS. Miscellaneous 170), ca. 1588–1603, five part-books, contains 20 textless works.

GB:CF (MS. D/DP.Z6/1), ca. 1590, contains works with incipits in all voices.

GB:T (MS. 1464), ca. 1590, two of original set of part-books, contains five-part instrumental music.

GB:Lbm (MS. Egerton 3665, 'Manuscript Musick'), late sixteenth century, contains 40 five-part instrumental works.

GB:Lbm (MS. DI. 24.d.2.), ca. 1580–1606, contains 14 Italian secular works, two with incipits and the others textless, and 44 additional instrumental or textless works.

GB:Ob (MS. Tenbury 1018), late sixteenth or early seventeenth centuries, contains 10 textless works, 1 In nomine, and 1 dance.

GB:Ob (MS. Tenbury 389), ca. 1595–1613, contains 23 textless works.

Print Collections Designated for Winds

Holborne, Antony

Pavans, Galliards, Almains, and other short Aeirs both grave, and light, in five parts, for Viols, Violins, or other Musicall Winde Instruments. The use of 'or other' here is the not uncommon Elizabethan usage meaning 'or else.' It is generally accepted that most of these works were first composed for the wind band of Sir Richard Champernowne.[1] (London: William Barley, 1599) Copies in GB: Och, and US:Cn. Contents and folio numbers:

[1] Andrew Kazdin, Cover Notes, 'The Glorious Sound of Brass,' Columbia Records (MS 6941).

[A3]	*Bona Speranza*
[A3]	*The teares of the Muses*
[A3v]	*Pavan*
[A3v]	*Lullabie*
[A4]	*The Cradle*
[A4]	*The New-yeeres gift*
[A4v]	*Pavan*
[A4v]	*The Marie-golde*
[B1]	*Pavan*
[B1]	*Galliard*
[B1v]	*Pavan*
[B1v]	*Galliard*
[B2]	*Pavan*
[B2]	*Galliard*
[B2v]	*Pavan*
[B2v]	*Galliard*
[B3]	*Paradizo*
[B3]	*The Sighes*
[B3v]	*Sedet Sola*
[B3v]	*Galliard*
[B4]	*Infernum*
[B4]	*Galliard*
[B4v]	*Spero*
[B4v]	*Galliard*
[C1]	*Patiencia*
[C1]	*Hermoza*
[C1v]	*The image of Melancholly*
[C1v]	*Ecce quam bonum*
[C2]	*Mens innovata*

[C2]	*Galliard*
[C2v]	*The funerals*
[C2v]	*Galliard*
[C3]	*Heres paternus*
[C3]	*Muy linda*
[C3v]	*Decrevi*
[C3v]	*My selfe*
[C4]	*Pavan*
[C4]	*Galliard*
[C4v]	*Pavan*
[C4v]	*Galliard*
[D1]	*Pavan*
[D1]	*Galliard*
[D1v]	*Amoretta*
[D1v]	*Nec invideo*
[D2]	*Pavan*
[D2]	*Galliard*
[D2v]	*Pavan*
[D2v]	*Galliard*
[D3]	*Pavana Ploravit*
[D3]	*Sic semper soleo*
[D3v]	*Galliard Posthuma*
[D3v]	*Galliard*
[D4]	*Last will and testament*
[D4]	*Galliard*
[D4v]	*The night watch*
[D4v]	*Almayne*
[E1]	*Almaine*
[E1]	*The fruit of love*
[E1]	*The Choise*
[E1v]	*The Honie-suckle*
[E1v]	*Wanton*
[E1v]	*The widowes myte*
[E1v]	*The Fairie-round*
[E2]	*As it fell on a holie Eve*
[E2]	*Heigh ho holiday*

Print Collections Without Instrument Designation

The whole psalmes in foure parts, whiche may be song to al musicall instrumentes, set forth for the encrease of vertue: and abolishing of other vayne and trifling ballades. (London: J. Day, 1563, four part-books) Copies in GB:Lu, and GB:Obc. The print contains 146 works by Brimle (11), Causton (27), Edwards, Hake (18), Parson (83), Shepherd, Southerton, and T. Tallis.

In this boke ar conteynyd xx songes ix of iiii partes, and xi of thre partes. (London, 1530) Copies in GB:Lbm (complete bassus and fol. 1 of triplex) and GB:Lwa (medius, fols. 1 and 45). Contents and folio numbers:

(iiii partes)

[A1]	*Pater noster* (Cornysh)
[A4]	*By by Pygot*
[C2]	*She may be callyd* (Ashwell)
[C3v]	*The bella* (Travenar)
[H1v]	*My love mournyth* (Gwynneth)
[J1]	*Pleasure it is* (Cornysh)
[J1v]	*Concordans musycall* (Cornysh)
[K2]	*Ut re my fa sol la* (Fayrfax) [textless]
[L3]	*Ut re my fa sol la* (Cowper) [textless]

(iii partes)

[A2]	*In youth* (Cowper)
[B1v]	*Beware my lytyll fynger*
[D2v]	*So great unkyndnes* (Cowper)
[E1v]	*Who shall have my fayr lady* (Jones)
[E3]	*Mynyon goo trym*
[F1v]	*Joly felow Joly*
[F3v]	*And wyl ye serve me soo*
[G1v]	*My harte my mynde* (Tavernar)
[G4v]	*Love wyll I* (Travernar)
[J3]	*My hartes lust* (Fayrfax)
[L1]	*Fa la soll* (Cornyshe) [textless]

Single Title Manuscripts Designated for Winds

Coprario, John (c. 1570–1626)

Verse, for cornett, sackbutt, and organ. Copy in US:NYp (Drexel MS. 5469, cornett and sackbut missing)

Single Title Manuscripts Without Instrument Designation

Ashton, Hugh (d. 1522)

Hornpype, GB:Lbm (MS. 26)

Blancks, Edward (ca. 1550–1633)

Motet, 'Credo quod Redemptor,' in twelve parts without text. GB:Lbm (MS).

Ferrabosci, 'young'

Pavana, a 4 note. GB:Lbm (MS Add. 29.372-7)

Holborne (d. 1602)

(Single Titles) found in a collection in GB:Cu, contents which have no instrumental designation (other manuscripts in this collection are marked 'viol Music'):

Allmaines (Id.2.11.f.70; Id.4.23.ff.9.13.16.)
Countess of Pembrokes Paradise (Id.9.33.f.70)
Cradle of Conceits (Add. 3056f.iv)
Fancy ded. Lord Borough (Id.4.23.f.3v)
Fantazias (Id.2.11.ff.27.28; Id.4.23.f.16)
Farewell (Id.2.11.f.63v; Id.3.18.f.18; Id.5.20.f.6; Id.5.21.f.3; Id.14.24.f.10v)
Galliards (Id.2.11.f.89; Id.4.23.f.12; Id.9.33.f.67)
Ground (Id.2.11.f.3v)
Jest (Id.2.11.f.60v)
Last Will and Testament (Id.2.11.f.32)
Passemeasure (Id.4.23.f.3)
Passemeasure Pavan (Id.4.23.f.17)
Passion (Id.2.11.f.83)

Paven (Id.2.11.ff.69,88)
Playfellow (Id.2.11.f.33; Id.5.78[III]ff.49v,51)
Ploravit (Id.2.11.f.10)
Cuadro Paven (Id.2.11.f.70v)
Response (Id.9.33.f.52)
Sedit sola (Id.2.11.f.43v)
Thought (Id.14.24.f.28)
Tres Choses (Id.2.11.f.36; Id.4.23.f.10)
Wanton (Id.9.33.f.67)

Holborn, A.

Galliarde, DDR:Dlb (MS. 1030 B1.62)

(Four) *Tanz*, for five instruments, collection printed by Füllsack. (Hamburg, 1607) Copy in BRD:W

FRANCE

Manuscript Collections Designated for Winds

F:Pn (MS. Rés. F. 494), *Music for Marriages, Coronations and other Sacred Events of Francois I, Henry III, Henry IV, and Louis XIII.*

This volume, part of the great Philidor collection, seems to have escaped the attention of persons interested in wind band music in France. In addition to the works given below, there are a large number of two-part dances, which I believe represent the period of Francois 1, 1515–1547.

Nr. 100 *Concert des grand hautbois pour les chevaliers fait par Henry III*, 1574–1589.

Nr. 101 *Air des grand hautbois pour les chevaliers fait par Henry III*.

Probable sixteenth century works:

Page 4. *Charivaris*, for unspecified five-parts.
Page 7. *Autre Charivaris de la St Julien*, in five-parts (the wind instrument guild in Paris was called, 'St Julien').
Page 8. *2d Air de la St Julien*.
Page 21. *Gaillard*, incomplete, for five-parts.

Manuscript Collections Without Instrument Designation

F:Pn (MS. Rés.F.496), *Airs*, Reign of Henry III [music of 1575–1583], *Dances*, Reign of Henry IV [music of 1598–1610], contains dance music in two, four, and five-parts.

F:Pn (MS. fonds fr. 1597), sixteenth century, includes three-part compositions with text incipits in one voice and incipits in the remaining two.

DK:Kk (MS. Ny Kongelige Samling 1848, 2), ca. 1525, Lyons, contains 1 instrumental work with an Italian title and 23 textless polyphonic works (2 with French and 8 with German secular concordances).

F:Pn (MS. Rés. 30345 A), ca. 1536–1540, Paris, includes 1 instrumental composition.

Print Collections Designated for Winds

Chansons musicales a quatre parties desquelles les plus convenables a la fleuste ... (Paris: Attaingnant, 1533) Copy in CH:LAcu

[1v]	*Per ch'el viso d'amour portava insegna*
[2]	Gombert, *J'aymeray qui m'aymera sans mélencolie*
[2v]	Testa, *O passi sparsi, O pensier vaghi e pronti*
[3v]	Jannequin, *Or vien ça, vien, m'amie Perrette*
[4v]	Certon, *Je l'ay ayme et l'aymeray le mien amy*
[5]	Guyon, *De noz deux cueurs soit seulle voulenté*
[5v]	Certon, *Si par fortune avez mon cueur acquis*
[6]	Manchicourt, *Désir m'assault et m'adresse la mort*
[6v]	Bourguignon, *O desloialle dame, la sourse de rigueur*
[7]	Gombert, *En espoir d'avoir mieulx il faut avoir souffranee*
[7v]	*Aultre que vous de moy ne jouyra*
[8]	Jacotin, *J'ay tant souffert que pour plaisir avoir*
[8v]	Gombert, *Hors envieux, retirez-vous d'ici*
[9]	Richafort, *Sur tous regretz les miens plus piteulz pleurent*
[9v]	Lupus, *Vostre beaulté plaisant et lyé*
[10]	Lupi, *Puis que j'ay perdu mes amours*
[10v]	Adorne, *Vous l'artés s'il vous plaist madame*
[11v]	J. Lemaire, *Mille regretz de vous abandonner*

[11v] Benedictus, *Le printemps faict florir les arbres par nature*
[12] Claudin, *Si ung oeuvre parfaict doibt chacum contenter*
[12v] Bridam, *Faict ou failly, ou du tout rien qui vaille*
[13] *Eslongné suys de mes amours*
[13v] Claudin, *Content desir qui cause ma douleur*
[13v] Claudin, *Vivre ne puys content sans sa présence*
[14] *Veu le grief mal ou sans repos labeure*
[14v] Benedictus, *Par trop aymer j'ay cuid' demourer*
[15] *La plus gorgiase du monde, le bruit, l'honneur*
[15v] Lupi, *Changer ne puys et aultre ne désire*
[16v] Heurteurs, *Souvent Amour me ... grant tourment*
[16v] Le Gendre, *Si je ne dors je ne puis vivre*

Vingt a sept chansons musicales a quatre parties desquelles les plus convenables a la fleuste ... (Paris: Attaingnant, 1533) Copies in CH:LAcu and BRD:Mbs (Mus. Pr. 31/5)

[1v] Claudin, *De vous servir m'est prins envie*
[1v] Heurteur, *Mirelaridon don don don daine*
[2v] Claudin, *Parle qui veult, tien seray j'en suys la*
[3] Passereau, *Va mirelidrogue va quent m'en venoys*
[3v] *A Paris prez des billetes, gentil maréschal*
[4] Vermont, *Les yeulx bendez de triste congnoissance*
[4v] Gombert, *Amours vous me faictes grant tort*
[5] Claudin, *Amour me poingt et si je me veulx plaindre*
[5v] Heurteur, *Allons ung peu plus avant, demourrons*
[6v] Heurteur, *Je ne puis pas mon grant deul appaiser*
[7] Passereau, *Tous amoureux qui hantés le commun*
[7v] Heurteur, *Par ung matin fuz levé devant le jour*
[8] P. de Manchicourt, *Pren de bon cueur le petit don que ton povre amy*
[8v] Heurteur, *Héllas, Amour qui sçais certainement*
[9] Claudin, *Amour me voyant sans tristesse*
[9v] Lupi, *Jeactés moy sur l'herbette mon amy gratieulx*
[10] Lupi, *Jamais ung cueur qui est d'amour embrasé ab*
[10v] Heurteur, *Troys jeunes bourgeoises aux Cordeliers s'en vont*
[11] Claudin, *Allez souspirs enflammez au froid cueur*
[11v] Claudin, *Elle veult donc par estrange rigueur*
[12] Vermont, *On dit qu'Amour luy mesmes l'aymera*
[12v] Jacotin, *Voyant souffrir celle qui me tourmente*
[13] Vermont, *Hayne et amour dedans mon cueur se tiennent*
[13v] Passereau, *Pour quoy donc ne fringuerons nous*
[14v] Passereau, *Je n'en diray mot, bergere m'amye*

[15]   Claudin, *Je n'avoye point a bien choisir failli*
[15v] Passereau, *Ung petit coup m'amye, ung petit coup, héllas*
[16v] Jacotin, *Si bon amour mérite récompense*

PRINT COLLECTIONS DESIGNATED FOR ANY INSTRUMENT

Six gaillardes et six pavanes avec treze chansons musicales a quatre parties ... (Paris: Attaingnant, [1530]) Copy in BRD:Mbs (Mus. Pro 31/1); modern print: Pariser Tanzbuch (European American Music, 1943).

[1v]   *Gaillarde 1*
[1v]   *Gaillarde 2*
[2]   *Gaillarde 3*
[2v]   *Gaillarde 4*
[2v]   *Gaillarde 5*
[3]   *Gaillarde 6*
[3v]   *Pavane 1*
[3v]   *Pavane 2*
[4]   *Pavane 3*
[4]   *Pavane 4*
[4v]   *Pavane 5*
[4v]   *Pavane 6*

Neuf basses dances deux branles vingt et cinq Pavannes avec quinze Gaillardes en musique a quatre parties ... (Paris: Attaingnant, 1530) Copies in BRD:Mbs (Mus. Pro 31/2); CH:LAcu ('Le X Livre'), and four of the pavanes in early manuscript in BRD:Mbs (Ms. Mus e 1516, Nrs. 185–188).

[1v]   *1 Basse dance*
[1v]   *2 Basse dance*
[2]   *3 Basse dance*
[2]   *4 La gatta en italien Basse dance*
[2v]   *5 La scarpa my faict mal Basse dance*
[3]   *6 La magdalena Basse dance Tourdion*
[3v]   *8 Basse dance*
[3v]   *9 La brosse Basse dance*
[4v]   *1 Branle*
[4v]   *2 Branle*
[5]   *1 Pavenne*
[5]   *2 Pavenne*

[5v]	3	*Pavenne*
[5v]	4	*Pavenne*
[6]	5	*Pavenne*
[6v]	6	*Pavenne*
[7]	7	*Pavenne*
[7v]	8	*Pavenne*
[7v]	9	*Pavenne*
[8]	10	*Pavenne*
[8]	11	*Pavenne*
[8v]	12	*Pavenne*
[8v]	13	*Pavenne*
[9]	14	*Pavenne*
[9]	15	*Pavenne*
[9v]	16	*Pavenne*
[9v]	17	*Pavenne*
[10]	18	*Pavenne Scd's superius*
[10v]	19	*Pavenne*
[11]	1	*Gaillarde*
[11v]	2	*Gaillarde*
[11v]	3	*Gaillarde*
[12]	4	*Gaillarde*
[12v]	5	*Gaillarde*
[12v]	6	*Gaillarde*
[13]	7	*Gaillarde*
[13]	8	*Gaillarde*
[13v]	9	*Gaillarde*
[13v]	10	*Gaillarde*
[14]	11	*Gaillarde*
[14v]	12	*Gaillarde*
[14v]	13	*Gaillarde*
[15]	14	*Gaillarde*
[15v]	15	*Gaillarde*
[15v]	20	*Pavenne*
[16]	21	*Pavenne*
[16]	22	*Pavenne*
[16]	23	*Pavenne*
[16v]	24	*Pavenne*
[16v]	25	*Pavenne La rote de rode*

Second livre contenant trois Gaillardes, TROIS PAVANES, VIGNT TROIS BRANLES, tant gays, Simples, Que doubles, Douze basses dances, & Neuf tourdions ... (Paris: Attaingnant, 1547) Copy in F:Pn (Rés. Vm 7. 376 [2]) Modern editions, Edition Moeck (Heft 3) and London Pro Musica

[1v]   *Basse dance*
[1v]   *Basse dance*
[2v]   *Basse dance*
[3v]   *Basse dance*
[4v]   *Basse dance. Celle qui m'a le nom damy donné.*
[5v]   *Basse dance. La volunté*
[6v]   *Tourdion*
[6v]   *Tourdion*
[7v]   *Tourdion*
[7v]   *Tourdion*
[8v]   *Branle simple*
[8v]   *Branle commun*
[9v]   *Tourdion*
[9v]   *Branle*
[10v] *Branle*
[10v] *Branle*
[11v] *Branle*
[11v] *Branle*
[12v] *Basse dance*
[12v] *Branle. L'espoir que jay.*
[13v] *Branle*
[13v] *Branle. Mari je songeois l'autre jour.*
[14v] *Branle*
[14v] *Branle de bourgoigne*
[15v] *Branle*
[15v] *Branle de champaigne*
[16v] *Branle*
[16v] *Branle*
[17v] *Basse dance. Aupres de vous*
[18v] *Tourdion. C'est grand plaisir*
[19v] *Tourdion. Vous aurez tout ca. qui est myen*
[20v] *Basse dance*
[21v] *Basse dance. Content désir*
[22v] *Basse dance. Par fin despit*

[23v] *Branle*
[24v] *Branle gay. Que je chatoulle ta fossette*
[25v] *Branle*
[25v] *Basse dance. Trop de regretz*
[26v] *Tourdion*
[26v] *Tourdion*
[27v] *Branle*
[27v] *Branle gay*
[28v] *Branle*
[28v] *Branle*
[29v] *Pavane*
[29v] *Pavane*
[30v] *Pavane*
[31v] *Gaillarde*
[31v] *Gaillarde*
[32v] *Gaillarde*

Premier livre des chansons esleues en nombre XXX. Pour les meilleures et plus frequentes, es cours des princes, convenables a tous instrumentz musicaulz. Nouvellement recoligées de plusieurs livres par cy devant imprimez dont aulcunes ont esté rechangées et mises au lieu des plus vielles et sont beaucop plus corectes que les precedentes. (Paris: Attaingnant, 1549) Copy in I:Fc (Basevi 2496/3).

[1v] Claudin, *Mon cueur voulut dedans soy recepvoir*
[1v] Certon, *Le voyr, l'ouyr, le parler, l'attoucher*
[2v] Sandrin, *Doulce mémoire en plaisir consomée*
[2v] Certon, *Finy le bien, le mal soudain commence*
[3v] Sandrin, *Ce qui souloit en deux se départir*
[3v] Claudin, *Amour est bien de perverse nature*
[4v] Claudin, *N'espoir ne paour n'auray jour de ma vie*
[4vl] Le moyne, *Le mal que j'ay rigueur le me procure*
[5v] De la Rue, *D'un desplaisir que fortune m'a faict*
[5v] Regnes, *Comme inconstante et de cueur faulse et lasche*
[6v] Bourguinon, *Continuer je veuil ma fermeté*
[6v] Pagnier, *Passions et douleurs qui suyvez tous malheurs*
[7v] Magdelain, *Sans liberté qu'un bon esprit regrete*
[7v] De villiers, *Veu le grief mal que longuement j'endure*
[8v] Certon, *O doulx revoir que mon esprit contente*
[8v] Claudin, *Amour me poingt et si je me veulx plaindre*
[9v] De villiers, *Force d'amour souvent me vault contraindre*

[10v] Claudin, *En espérant en ceste longue attente*
[10v] Claudin, *Contentez-vous, amy, de la pensée*
[11v] Mittantier, *Plus je la vois moins y trouve a redire*
[11v] Hesdin, *Plaindre l'ennuy de la peine estimee*
[12v] Claudin, *Vous perdex temps de me dire mal d'elle*
[12v] Mittantier, *Tel ne mesdit qui pour soy la désire*
[13v] Heurteur, *Hélas, Amour qui sçais certainement*
[13v] Sandrin, *Si mon travail vous peult donner plaisir*
[14v] De Villiers, *Le dueil issu de la joye incertaine*
[14v] Sandrin, *Puis que de vous je n'ay aultre visaige*
[15v] Certon, *Ung moins aymant aura peult estre mieux*
[15v] Godard, *Hélas Amour, je pensoye bien avoir*
[16v] Morel, *Est-il possible que l'on puisse trouver*

Second livre contenant XXIX chansons, esleues pour les meilleures et plus frequenstes es cours des princes convenables à tous instrumentz musicaluz ... (Paris: Attaingnant, 1549) Copy in I:Fc (Basevi 2496/4).

[1v] Certon, *M'amye un jour le Dieu Mars désarma*
[1v] Boyvin, *Je cherche autant amour et le désire*
[2v] Certon, *Frere Thibault, séjourne, gros et gras*
[3v] Certon, *En fut-il oncques une plus excellente*
[3v] Claudin, *Comment puis-je ma déspartie*
[4v] Certon, *O triste adieu qui tant me mescontente*
[4v] Certon, *O comme heureux t'estimeroys mon cueur*
[5v] Sandrin, *Ce qui est plus en ce monde amyable*
[5v] Claudin, *Amour, voyant l'ennuy qui tant m'oppresse*
[6v] De villiers, *Rien n'est plus cher que ce que l'on désire*
[6v] Belin, *Plus je le voy de beaucoup estimé*
[7v] Sandrin, *Voulant honneur que de vous je m'absente*
[7v] Claudin, *Je n'ay poinct plus d'affection*
[8v] Sandrin, *Hélas amy, je congnois bien que ne puis nyer mon*
[8v] Sandrin, *La voulunté si longtemps endormie*
[9v] Constantius Festa, *O passi sparsi, O pensier vaghi e pronti*
[10v] Sandrin, *Je ne le croy et le scay seurement*
[10v] Sandrin, *Si vostre amour ne gist qu'en apparance*
[11v] Harchadelt, *Au temps heureulx que ma jeune ignorance*
[11v] Maillard, *Si mon vouloir ne change de désir*
[12v] Maillard, *Au feu, venez moy secourir*
[12v] Maillard, *Hélas mon Dieu, ton yre c'est tournée*
[13v] Boyvin, *Je sentz l'affection qui a moy se vient rendre*

[13v]	D'Auxerre, *Oeil pleu constant, messagier de pensées*
[14v]	Sandrin, *Ce qui m'est deu et ordonné*
[14v]	Sandrin, *Pleurez mes yeulx, pour la dure déffense qui rend*
[15v]	Gardane, *La palme doulce avant que feuilles rendre*
[15v]	Belin, *Si l'on me monstre affection*
[16v]	De la font, *Ung advocat dict a se femme*

Tiers livre contenant XXVIII chansons esleues pour les meilleures et plus frequentes es cours des princes. Convenables à tous instrumentz musicaulx ... (Paris: Attaingnant, 1550) Copy in I:Fc (Basevi 2496/5). Modern edition, London Pro Musica AD3.

[1v]	Claudin, *Trop tost j'ay creu y prenant tel plaisir*
[1v]	Claudin, *O combien est malheureux le désir*
[2v]	Poillhiot, *Nostre amytié et nouvelle alliance*
[2v]	Claudin, *Or sus Amour, puisque tu m'as attaint*
[3v]	Claudin, *Je suys tant bien, voire tant bien encore*
[3v]	Sandrin, *Je ne puis bonnement penser*
[4v]	Sandrin, *Quant j'ay congneu en ma pensée*
[4v]	Godard, *Longtemps y a que langueur et tristesse*
[5v]	Vassal, *Vray Dieu tant j'ay le cueur gay*
[6v]	Maille, *Las, me fault-il tant de mal supporter*
[6v]	Jantian, *Celle qui a fascheux mary*
[7v]	Gombert, *Mort et fortune, pourquoy m'avez laissé*
[7v]	Cadeac (or Lupil), *Je suis déshéritée puisque j'ay perdu mon amy*
[8v]	Harcadel, *Il est vray que vostre oeil qui pleure, le mien tente*
[8v]	Certon, *De long travail heureuse récompense*
[9v]	Janequin, *Ouvrez-moy l'huys, hé Jehanneton m'amye*
[10v]	Certon, *Si j'ay eu tousjours mon vouloir*
[10v]	Sandrin, *Si pour t'aymer et désirer*
[11v]	Claudin, *Puis qu'il est tel qu'il garde bien s'amye*
[11v]	Certon, *O cueur ingrat qui tant m'est redebvable*
[12v]	Peletier, *Hélas Amour, tu feiz mal ton debvoir*
[12v]	Janequin, *Si de bon cueur j'ayme bien une dame*
[13v]	Certon, *De tout le mal que d'un vouloir constant*
[13v]	Rogier, *D'amour me plains et non de vous m'amye*
[14v]	Clemens, *Je prens en gré la dure mort*
[14v]	Goudeaul, *Dieu des amantz ton pouvoir est petit*
[15v]	Lupy, *Plus revenir ne puis vers toy ma dame*
[16v]	Lupy, *Reviens vers moy qui suis tant desolée*

Musicque de joye. Appropriée tant à la voix humaine, que pour apprendre a sonner espinetes, violons et fleustes ... (Lyon: J. Moderne, ca. 1550, in four part-books). Copy in BRD:Mbs. This volume consists of 22 ricercares (by Willaert, Segni, and others) and 29 anonymous dances.

Quart livre de danceries a quatre parties contenant XIX pavanes et XXXI gaillardes EN UNG LIVRE SEUL, VEU ET CORREIGE PAR Claude gervaise scavant Musicien ... (Paris: Attaingnant, 1550) Copies in F:Pn (Rés. Vm 7.376/3) and GB:Lbm. Modern editions: London Pro Musica (Nr. AD4 and Edition Moeck (Heft 4).

[1v]	*Pavance La venissienne*
[2v]	*Pavane*
[2v]	*Gaillarde*
[3v]	*Pavane*
[3v]	*Gaillarde*
[4v]	*Pavane L'oeil pres et loing*
[4v]	*Gaillarde*
[5v]	*Pavanne Vous qui voulez*
[5v]	*Gaillarde*
[6v]	*Pavane*
[6v]	*Gaillarde*
[7v]	*Pavane Qui souhaitez*
[7v]	*Gaillarde*
[8v]	*Pavane Plus revenir*
[8v]	*Gaillarde*
[9v]	*Pavane M'amyee est tant honneste et saige*
[9v]	*Gaillarde*
[10v]	*Pavane o foyble esprit*
[11v]	*Pavane Le bon vouloir*
[12v]	*Pavane*
[13v]	*Pavane Pour mon plaisir*
[14v]	*Pavane*
[15v]	*Pavane*
[16v]	*Pavane*
[17v]	*Pavane*
[18v]	*Pavne DELLESTARPE*
[19v]	*Pavane*
[20v]	*Gaillarde i*
[21v]	*Gaillarde ii*

[22v] *Gaillarde iii*
[23v] *Gaillarde iiii*
[24v] *Gaillarde v*
[25v] *Gaillarde vi*
[25v] *Gaillarde vii*
[25v] *Gaillarde viii*
[26v] *Gaillarde i*
[26v] *Gaillarde ii*
[27v] *Gaillarde iii*
[27v] *Gaillarde iv*
[27v] *Gaillarde v*
[28v] *Gaillarde vi*
[28v] *Gaillarde vii*
[28v] *Gaillarde viii*
[29v] *Gaillarde ix*
[29v] *Gaillarde x*
[29v] *Gaillarde xi*
[30v] *Gaillarde xii*
[30vl] *Gaillarde (xiii)*
[31v] *Gaillarde xiiii*
[31v] *Gaillarde (xv)*

Cinquiesme livre de danceries, A quatre PARTIES, CONTENANT DIX BRANSLES GAYS, Huict bransles de poictou, Trente cinq bransles de Champaigne, Le tout en ung livre seul, Veu & corrige par Claude gervaise scavant Musicien ... (Paris: Attaingnant, 1550). Copy in F:Pn (Rés. Vm 7.376/4). Modern editions London Pro Musica, AD 5, and Edition Moeck (Heft 4).

[1v] *Bransle gay i*
[1v] *Bransle gay ii*
[2v] *Bransle gay iii*
[2v] *Bransle gay iiii*
[3v] *Bransle gay v*
[3v] *Bransle gay vi*
[4v] *Bransle gay vii*
[4v] *Bransle gay viii*
[5v] *Bransle gay ix*
[5v] *Bransle gay x*
[6v] *Bransle de poictou i*
[6v] *Bransle de poictou ii*

[7v]	*Bransle de poictou iii*
[7v]	*Bransle de poictou iv*
[8v]	*Bransle de poictou v*
[9v]	*Bransle de poictou vi*
[10v]	*Bransle de poictou vii*
[10v]	*Bransle de poictou viii*
[11v]	*Bransle de champaigne i*
[12v]	*Bransle ii*
[12v]	*Bransle iii*
[13v]	*Bransle iiii*
[13v]	*Bransle v*
[14v]	*Bransle vi*
[15v]	*Bransle vii*
[15v]	*Bransle viii*
[16v]	*Bransle ix*
[16v]	*Bransle x*
[17v]	*Bransle xi*
[18v]	*Bransle de champaigne*
[19v]	*Bransle ii*
[19v]	*Bransle iii*
[20v]	*Bransle iiii*
[21v]	*Bransle v*
[21v]	*Bransle vi*
[22v]	*Bransle vii*
[23v]	*Bransle viii*
[24v]	*Bransle ix*
[24v]	*Bransle x*
[25v]	*Bransle xi*
[25v]	*Bransle xii*
[26v]	*Bransle xiii*
[26v]	*Bransle xiiii*
[27v]	*Bransle de champaigne*
[28v]	*Bransle ii*
[28v]	*Bransle iii*
[29v]	*Bransle iv*
[29v]	*Bransle v*
[30v]	*Bransle vi*
[30v]	*Bransle vii*
[31v]	*Bransle viii*
[31v]	*Bransle ix*
[31v]	*Bransle x*

Premier livre du recueil contenant XXX chansons anciennes, a quatre parties en un volume ... les plus convenables aux instrumens ... (Paris: N. du Chemin, 1551). Copy in F:Pn. The print contains 30 compositions by Berchem, Bourguignon, Certon (5), Clemens non papa, Godard, Jacotin, de La Rue, Lupus, Magdelain, Mittantier, Morel, Mornable, Regnes, Sandrin (5), Sermisy, and Villiers.

Premier livre du recueil, contenant XXVIII chansons anciennes, a quatre parties en quatsre volumes ... convenables aux instrumens ... (Paris: N. du Chemin, 1551). Copy in DDR:Bds (incomplete: T only) and F:Nd (incomplete: A only). The print contains 28 works by Berchem, Bourguignon, Certon (5), Clemens non papa, Godard, Jacotin, de La Rue, Lupus, Magdelain, Mittantier, Morel, Mornable, Sandrin (4), Sermisy, and Villiers.

Second livre du recueil, contenant XXVI chansons anciennes, a quatre parties en quatre volumes ... convenables aux instrumens ... par l'advis de bons, et scavantz musiciens ... (Paris, N. du Chemin, 1551). Copies in DDR:Bds (incomplete: T only), F:Nd (incomplete: A only), and F:Pn (incomplete: B only). The print contains 26 compositions by Arcadelt, Belin, Boyvin, Certon, Dauxerre, Delafont, Gardane, Goudeaul, Milliard, Marle, Sandriu (5), Santerre, Sermisy, Villiers, and anonymous.

Tiers livre de danceries (A and T lost, cited by Grove without source).

Quart livre du recueil, contenant XXVII chansons anciennes, a quatre parties, en un volume ... convenables aux instrumens ... par l'advis de bons, et scavantz musicians ... (Paris: N. du Chemin, 1551). Copy in F:Pn (mq.f. 16–32). The print contains 27 works by Arcadelt, Certon, Guyon, Jacotin, Janequin, Le Heurteur, Lupi, de Manchicourt, Mittantier, Roque lay, Sandrin, and Sermisy (11).

Quart livre du recueil, contenant XXVI chansons anciennes, a quatre parties en quatre volumes ... convenables aux instrumens ... par l'advis de bons et scavants musiciens ... (Paris: N. du Chemin, 1551). Copies in DDR:Bds (incomplete: T only) and F:Nd (incomplete: A only). The print contains 26 compositions by Arcadelt, Certon, Guyon, Jacotin, Janequin, Le Heurteur, Lupi, de Manchicourt, Mittantier, Roquelay, Sandrin, and Sermisy (11).

Sixieme livre de danceries, mis en musique a quatre parties par Claude Gervaise ... (Paris: Attaingnant, 1555). Copy in F:Pn (Rés. Vm 7.376/5). Modern edition: London Pro Musica, AD6

[1v]	*Pavane Passemaize*
[1v]	*Gaillarde*
[2v]	*Pavane des dieux*
[2v]	*Gaillarde des dieux*
[3v]	*Pavane d'Angleterre*
[3v]	*Gaillarde*
[4v]	*ii Gaillarde*
[4v]	*iii Gaillarde*
[4v]	*iiii Gaillarde*
[5v]	*v Gaillarde*
[5v]	*vi Gaillarde*
[6v]	*Fin de Gaillarde*
[7v]	*Bransle simple i*
[8v]	*Bransle simple ii*
[9v]	*Bransle de Champaigne i*
[9v]	*Bransle de Champaigne ii*
[10v]	*Bransle de Champaigne iii*
[10v]	*Bransle de Champaigne iiii*
[11v]	*Bransle de Champaigne v*
[11v]	*Bransle de Champaigne vi*
[12v]	*Bransle de Champaigne vii*
[12v]	*Bransle de Champaigne viii*
[13v]	*Bransle de Champaigne ix*
[13v]	*Bransle de Champaigne x*
[14v]	*Bransle de Champaigne xi*
[14v]	*Bransle de Champaigne xii*
[15v]	*Bransle courant i*
[16v]	*Bransle courant ii*
[17v]	*Bransle gay i*
[18v]	*Bransle gay ii*
[18v]	*Bransle gay iii*
[19v]	*Bransle simple i*
[20v]	*Bransle simple ii*

[21v]   *Bransle simple iii*
[21v]   *Bransle simple iv*
[22v]   *Bransle gay i*
[23v]   *Bransle gay ii*
[24v]   *Bransle de Champaigne i*
[24v]   *Bransle de Champaigne ii*
[25v]   *Bransle de Champaigne iii*
[25v]   *Bransle de Champaigne iiii*
[26v]   *Bransle de Champaigne v*
[26v]   *Bransle de Champaigne vi*
[27v]   *Bransle de Champaigne vii*
[27v]   *Bransle de Champaigne viii*
[28v]   *Bransle de Champaigne ix*
[28v]   *Bransle de Champaigne x*
[29v]   *Bransle de Champaigne xi*
[29v]   *Bransle de Champaigne xii*
[30v]   *Bransle gay i*
[30v]   *Bransle gay ii*
[31v]   *Bransle gay iii*
[31v]   *Bransle gay iiii*

TROISIEME LIVRE DE DANCERIES A QUATRE ET CINQ PARTIES, VEU PAR CLAUDE Gervaise (Ie tout en un volume) … (Paris: Attaingnant, 1556). Copy in F:Pn (Rés. VII: 7.376/2). Modern Edition: London Pro Musica.

[1v]   *Pavanne, Si je m'en vois. A cinq.*
[1v]   *Gaillarde, Si je m'en vois*
[2v]   *Pavanne, Est-il conclud*
[3v]   *Gaillarde, Est-il conclud*
[4v]   *Pavanne, l'Admiral*
[4v]   *Gaillarde*
[5v]   *Pavanne de la guerre*
[7v]   *Gaillarde*
[8v]   *Gaillarde*
[8v]   *Gaillarde*
[8v]   *Gaillarde*
[8v]   *Gaillarde*
[9v]   *Bransle simple i*
[10y]   *Bransle simple ii*
[10vl] *Bransle simple iii*
[11v]   *Bransle simple iiii*

[12v] *Bransle simple v*
[12v] *Bransle simple vi*
[13v] *Bransle gay i*
[13v] *Bransle gay ii*
[14v] *Bransle gay iii*
[14v] *Bransle gay iiii*
[15v] *Bransle gay v*
[15v] *Bransle gay vi*
[16v] *Almande i*
[17v] *Almande ii*
[18v] *Almande iii*
[18v] *Almande iiii*
[19v] *Almande v*
[19v] *Almande vi*
[20v] *Almande vii*
[20v] *Et d'ou venez-vous madame Lucette, Almande viii*
[21v] *Bransle de Bourgogne i*
[22v] *Bransle ii*
[23v] *Bransle iii*
[24v] *Bransle iiii*
[24v] *Bransle v*
[25v] *Bransle vi*
[26v] *Bransle vii*
[27v] *Bransle viii*
[27v] *Bransle ix*
[28v] *Bransle x*
[29v] *Bransle i*
[29v] *Bransle ii*
[30v] *Bransle iii*
[30v] *Bransle iiii*
[31v] *Bransle v*
[31v] *Bransle vi*

SEPTIEME LIVRE DE DANCERIES, MIS EN MUSIQUE A QUATRE PARTIES par Estienne du Tertre ... (Paris: Attaingnant, 1557). Copy in F:Pn (Rés. Vm 7.376/6). Modern edition: London: Pro Musica, AD7.

[1v] *Pavane premiere*
[1v] *Gaillarde premiere*
[2v] *Pavane 2.*
[2v] *Gaillarde 2.*

    [3v]   *Pavane 3. (A cinq)*
    [4v]   *Gaillarde 3. A cinq*
    [5v]   *Pavane 4.*
    [5v]   *Gaillarde 4.*
    [6v]   *Pavane 5.*
    [6v]   *Gaillarde 5.*
    [7v]   *Pavane 6. A cinq*
    [8v]   *Gaillarde 6. A cinq*

Premiere suytte de Bransles

    [9v]   *Bransle 1.*
    [10v]   *Bransle 2.*
    [10v]   *Bransle 3.*
    [11v]   *Bransle 4.*
    [11v]   *Bransle 5.*

Seconde suytte de Bransles

    [12v]   *Bransle 1.*
    [l2v]   *Bransle 2.*
    [13v]   *Bransle 3.*
    [13v]   *Bransle 4.*
    [14v]   *Bransle 5.*
    [14v]   *Bransle 6.*

Troisieme suytte de Bransles

    [15v]   *Bransle 1.*
    [15v]   *Bransle 2.*
    [16v]   *Bransle 3.*
    [16v]   *Bransle 4.*
    [17v]   *Bransle 5.*
    [17v]   *Bransle 6.*

Premiere suytte de Bransles d'Escosse

    [18v] *Premier Bransle d'Escosse*
    [18v] *Bransle 2.*
    [19v] *Bransle 3.*
    [19v] *Bransle 4.*

Table:

    Seconde suytte de bransles d'Escosse xxi
    Six bransles de Poictou xxiij

Huict bransles gays xxvj
Cinq Gaillardes xxix

PREMIER LIVRE DE DANSERIES, Contenat 14 Bransles Communs. 16 Bransles Gays. 20 Bransles de Champaigne. 6 Autres Bransles de Champaigne legiers. 1 Autre Bransle appellé le petit gentilhomme. 1 Autre Bransle des Lavandieres. Le tout mis en Musique à quatre parties (appropriés tan à la voix humaine, que pour jouer sur tous instruments musicalz) Par Jean d'Estrée, joueur de Hautbois du Roy. (Paris: Nicolas du Chemin, 1559, in four part-books). Copies in F:Psg (incomplete: S only) and GB:Lbm (incomplete: B only). This publication, by a member of the king's wind band is almost certainly taken from the repertoire of that ensemble.

SECOND LIVRE DE DANSERIES, Contenant 18 Bransles de Bourgongne. 1 Bransle de Bourgongne legier. 18 Bransles de Poitou. 7 Bransles d'Escosse. 1 Bransle appellé le Bransle des Sabots. 9 Bransles de la Guerre. 1 Bransle appellé la Tireteinne. 1 Autre Bransle appellé le petit Velours. Le tout mis en Musique à quatre parties (appropriés tant à la voix humaine, que pour jouer sur tous instruments musicalz) Par Jean d'Estrée, joueur de Hautbois du Roy. (Paris, Nicolas du Chemin, 1559, in four part-books). Copies in F:Psg (incomplete: S only) and GB:Lbm (incomplete: B only).

TIERS LIVRE DE DANSERIES, Contenant
5 Bransles de Malthe.
1 Le pas meige.
1 La Padouenne.
4 Tintelores.
1 Les Bouffons.
10 Allemandes.
1 Bransle de la torche.
1 Bransle de Montirande.
3 Ballets du Canat.
1 La volte de Prouvence.
3 Pavanes à 4, & à 6.
8 Gaillardes à 4, & à 5.
5 Basse danses.
1 Hauberrois.

Le tout mis en Musique à quatre parties (appropriés tant à la voix humaine, que pour jouer sur tous instruments musicalz) Par Jean d'Estrée, joueur de Hautbois du Roy. (Paris: Nicolas du Chemin, 1559, in four part-books). Copies in F:Psg (incomplete, S only) and GB:Lbm (incomplete, B only).

QUART LIVRE DE DANSERIES, Contenant
  5 Pavanes, avec leurs Gaillardes à 4. & à 5. parties
  1 Gaillarde ditte la Visdame
  1 Autre a 5. ditte la Milannoise
  1 Autre Gaillarde à 5.
  1 Le Bal de Calais à 5. parties
  1 La basse Gaillarde à 4.
  3 Bransles des contrainctz
  4 Bransles de Poictou, simples & legeirs
  1 Le Bransle de Guillemette
  1 Le Bransle du petit homme
  1 Bransle legeir double du p.h.
  4 Alemandes

Le tout mis en Musique à 4. à 5. & à 6. parties (appropriés tant à la voix humaine, que pour jouer sur tous instruments musicaulz) Par Jean d'Estrée, joueur de Hautbois du Roy. (Paris Nicolas du Chemin, 1564, in four part-books). Copy in GB:Lbin (incomplete, only B).

Beaujoyeulx, Ballthasar de

BALET COMIQUE DE LA ROYNE, FAICT AUX NOPCES DE MONsieur le Duc de Joyeuse ... (Paris: Le Roy, Ballard & Patisson, 1582). Copies in A:Wn; F:B, Nd, Pa, Pn, Pm, Po, Pthibault, and RO; GB:Lbm; I:Tn; NL:DHgm; US:CA, NYp, SM, U, and Wc. Composed for a court entertaimnent during the reign of Henry III, this volume contains five instrumental compositions, four in five-parts and one (Nr. 3) in twelve-parts.

[27v] *La premiere entrée*
[30v] *Le son de la clochete, auquel Circé sortie de son Jardin*
[42v] *Response de la voute dorée aux vertus: à chaque couplet c'estoit une Musique de douze instrumens sans voix.*

[56v] *La petite entrée du grand balet*
[56v] *La grand'entrée*

Arbeau, Thoinot

Orchésographie (Langres: J. des Preyz, 1588). This famous, and often reprinted, treatise on dancing contains the complete melodies for 44 dances and one complete pavan in four-parts.

Single Title Prints Designated for Any Instrument

Colin, Pierre

Les cinq. uante pseaulmes de David ... le tout mis en musique ... à quatre parties en quatre volumes en chant non vulgaire: mais plus convenable aux instrumens. (Paris: Nicolas du Chemin, 1550). Copy in F:Pn (incomplete, S only).

Caietain (Cajetan), Fabrice Martin (fl. 1570–1578)

Liber primus (Paris, 1571). Copy in B:Br (incomplete). A collection of four-voice motets dedicated to the canons of Toul Cathedral. The title stresses the suitability for instruments.[2]

[2] See Grove, 3:607.

Single Title Prints Without Instrument Designation

Cordeilles, Charles (fl. Lyons 1540–1548)

Au despourveu le non voyant gecta (1540). Copies in BRD:Mbs and GB:Lbm. This chanson, and the following ones, were composed by the leader of the Lyons civic wind band, which in 1548 consisted of nine shawms, dolcians, cornetts, and a sordun. The simple style of these four-part chansons suggest a possible relationship with this civic band's repertoire.

Doulx preférer de bouche tant heureuse (1540). Copies in BRD:Mbs and GB:Lbm.

May gratieux reverdissant (1540). Copies in BRD:Mbs and GB:Lbm.

Mes durs ennuys fontaine ont seichée (1540). Copies in BRD:Mbs and GB:Lbm.

GERMANY

MANUSCRIPT COLLECTIONS DESIGNATED FOR WINDS

DK:Kk (MS. Gamle kongelige Samling, 1872/4), ca. 1541–1543, in seven part-books, consists of 149 polyphonic works with text incipits only, including an eight-part motet for cornetts and trombones; 13 works called, 'Fuga'; and 3 textless works. Individual works are dedicated to Christian III, and the German Dukes, Albert of Prussia, Heinrich of Brunswick, and Friedrich I of Saxony. This is one of the most important early band documents and is generally taken to represent the wind band library of Duke Albert of Prussia.

MANUSCRIPT COLLECTIONS WITHOUT INSTRUMENT DESIGNATION

BRD:B (MS. 40194, Part II), sixteenth century, contains 26 French, 3 Italian, and 2 German secular works with text incipits only and 3 textless compositions.

BRD:B (MS. 40027) [lost, according to Grove], a score which contains a five-part textless composition by Christian Erbach.

BRD:B (MS. 40195, Part I), sixteenth century, contains 20 French and 2 German works with incipits only and 1 textless composition.

BRD:Mbs (MS. 3156), first-half, sixteenth century, contains 1 textless composition.

CH:SAM (MS. M. 30–31), two of the original four part-books, first-half, sixteenth century manuscript from middle or Eastern Germany, contains 3 textless works.

DDR:GRu (MS. Eb 133), early sixteenth century, two of four original part-books which contained only text incipits in all voices.

BRD:Rtt (MS. Freie Künste Musik 3/1), early sixteenth century, perhaps from a monastery in Neresheim, contains 3 textless works.

PL:Wu (MS. Mf. 2016), ca. 1500–1517, Silesia or perhaps Bohemia, contains 2 textless motets, 2 textless hymns, and 7 other textless polyphonic works.

BRD:As (MS. 2/142a) , ca. 1505–1514, a choirbook which contains several anonymous instrumental works, including three- and four-part dances ('*Passamezzo moderno*' [f20], '*Mantuanner dantz de schallter cel*' [f18v], '*La monina*' [f20v], etc.).

BRD:As (MS. Ink. 529), ca. 1507–1510, from Southern Bavaria, contains 10 textless polyphonic compositions.

DDR:Dlb (MS. l/D/505), ca. 1510–1530, contains 166 compositions of which 3 are textless.

DDR:Dlb (MS. 1/D/506), ca. 1510–1530, contains 162 compositions of which 1 is textless.

PL:WRu (MS. I.F.428), ca. 1510–1530, middle or Eastern German, or perhaps Frankfurt, contains 7 textless polyphonic compositions.

BRD:Mbs (MS. 4483), ca. 1515, South German, contains 3 textless polyphonic compositions.

BRD:Rp (MS. C. 120), before ca. 1522, South German or Austrian, a choirbook containing more than 100 compositions of which more than three-quarters are textless.

BRD:Mu (MS. 80/328–331), four of the original five part-books, ca. 1523–1530, probably from Munich, contains 14 textless compositions, mostly entitled, '*Carmen.*'

BRD:Rtt (MS. Freie Künste Musik 76 Abth. II), ca. 1530–1538, Saxony, contains 1 textless work called '*Hymnus.*'

DDR:Z (MS. LXXVIII, 2), four part-books, 1531, contains polyphonic textless compositions.

F:Pn (MS. Rés. Vm 7.504 [incomplete, S only]), ca. 1532–1535, consists of three anonymous collections of part-books entirely without text, except for text incipits.

BRD:KA (MS. 80 Mus. 53/2), one of three original part-books, ca. 1534–1546, court of Philip of Hesse, contains 1 motet without text, 2 French secular compositions without text, and 5 textless works.

BRD:KA (MS 40/Mus. 38/1–6) six part-books, ca. 1535–1566, court of Philip of Hesse, contains 15 textless compositions, 7 with Latin, 4 with German, and 2 with French text incipits.

CH:Zz (MS. Q. 906), after 1536, German, contains 1 composition with an uncertain text incipit.

BRD:Mbs (MS. 1516), ca. 1540, South German, four part-books containing 161 compositions, all but one without text.

DDR:Z (MS. LXXXVI ,3) , three part-books, 1542, includes 2 motets without text.

BRD:B (MS. 40043 [lost]), four part-books, ca. 1542–1544, Torgau, included 1 textless work.

BRD:Mbs (MS. 80/327), 1543, probably Augsburg, contains 1 textless composition.

BRD:ISL (MS. without shelf-mark), five part-books, 1544, German, either Augsburg or Nürnberg, contains 90 textless compositions.

DDR:Z . (MS. LXXVIII, 3), three part-books, before 1546, consists of 26 textless compositions.

DDR:Dlb (MS. Grimma 59/1–2), ca. 1550, contains 2 textless compositions.

BRD:Hs (MS. Hans. III, 4/1 [lost]), mid-sixteenth century, Hamburg, contains 1 instrumental dance.

BRD:HB (MS . X/2 [incomplete, B only]), early 1550s, perhaps Frankfurt, contains 31 textless compositions.

DDR:Dlb (MS. Pirna III), ca. 1550–1565, German, contains 1 textless composition.

DDR:Z (MS. CVI, 5), five part-books, 1554, consisting of 8 'songs,' without text.

DDR:LEu (MS. Thomaskirche 51), two of original four part-books, ca. 1555, contains 1 textless work.

BRD:Rtt (MS. A.R. 940–941), ca. 1552–1560, contains 314 compositions of which 17 are instrumental, 67 are French chansons without text and 31 are Italian madrigals without text. Even where there are incipits, they are frequently disfigured (as for example, '*Simon traval*' for '*Si mon travail*') suggesting that perhaps this manuscript was copied from another source than the originals. The manuscript also includes instrumental works, some called dances and some 'Gallicum,' by Othmayr, Finck, and Keutzenhoff, although most are anonymous.

BRD:Ud (MS. 237), 1557, contains three-part works with text in one voice and textless in the remaining two.

DDR:Dlb (MS. Löbau 51/1–3, part II), three part-books, ca. 1560–1570, Löbau, contains 1 textless composition.

DDR:Dlb (MS. Grimma 55/1–7), seven part-books, ca. 1560–1580, contains 3 textless polyphonic compositions.

DDR:Dlb (MS. Grimma 51/1–4), four part-books, ca. 1570–1580, contains 1 textless polyphonic composition.

BRD:Usch (MS. 236a-d), ca. 1570–1590, contains four-part instrumental dances.

DDR:Dlb (MS. Grimma 7/1–4), four part-books, ca. 1590–1621, contains 4 textless polyphonic compositions.

BRD:Lr (MS. Mus.Ant.Pract. K.N. 144/1–4), four part-books, ca. 1590, perhaps Braunschweig, contains 1 polyphonic textless composition.

DDR:Dlb (MS. Löbau 8 & Löbau 70), eight-part books, ca. 1592, Löbau, contains 1 polyphonic textless composition.

DDR:Dlb (MS. Lobau 14/1–5), five part-books, ca. 1600, Löbau, contains 1 polyphonic textless work.

BRD:B (MS. 40208), late-sixteenth century, contains many French, Italian and German secular works with text incipits only, together with 4 textless compositions.

BRD:B (MS.40028), ca. 1599–1617, a manuscript score containing three instrumental works, a five-part canzona by Erbach, an eight-part canzona by Bramieri, and a six-part, *'capriccio de cornetti,'* by Lichtlein.

S:Uu (MS. Vokalmusik i Randskrift 76b), Apparently late-sixteenth century, national source unclear, contains 8 textless polyphonic compositions.

Print Collections Designated for Winds

In dissem Buechlyn fynt man LXXV. hubscher Lieder myt Discant. Alt. Bass. und Tenor. lustick zu syngen. Auch etlich zu fleiten, schwegelen und an deren musicalisch Instrumenten artlichen zu gebrauchen (Köln: Arnt von Aich [c. 1519]). Copies in CH:Bu and BRD:B. The print contains 75 compositions by Adam von Fulda, Brack, Grefinger, Hofhaimer (3), Isaac, Lapicida, Pipelare, Rener, and 63 anonymous.

Orologio, Alexander

INTRADAE ALEXANDRI OROLOGII, quinque & sex vocibus ... (Helmaestadii: Jacobi Lucii, 1597). This collection of 28 intradas is known to have been composed for winds. Copies in BRD:Kl and DK:Kk. Six intradas from this collection are available in a modern edition by London Pro Musica.

Print Collections Designated for Any Instrument

Anonymous Compilers

Der erst Teil. Hundert und ainundzweintzig newe Lieder, von berumbtenn dieser Kunst gesetzt, lustig zu singen, und auff allerley Instrument dienstlich ... (Nürnberg: H.

Formschneider, 1534). Copies in BRD:Mbs and DDR:Z. Contains 120 compositions by Arnold von Bruck (20), Breitengraser (16), Senfl (81), and anonymous.

Schöne auszerlesne Lieder, des hoch berümpten Heinrici Finckens, sampt andern newen Liedern ... lustig zu singen, und auff die Instrument dienstlich ... (Nürnberg: H. Formschneider, 1536). Copies in BRD:Mbs and DDR:Z. The print contains 55 works by H. Finck (30), 'J .S.' [Schechinger?] (12), A. von Bruck, Mahu, and Senfl (9).

Trium vocum carmina (Nürnberg: Hieronymus Formschneider, 1538, in three part-books). These volumes contain 100 three-part works without text. Copies in BRD:Bhm and DDR:Ju.

Ein Ausszug guter alter und newer teutscher Liedlein, einer rechten teutschen Art, auff allerley Instrumenten zubrauchen ... (Nürnberg, J. Petreius, 1539). Copies in BRD:Mbs; DDR:Ju and Z. The print contains 130 works by von Bruck, Blanckmuller, Bohemus, Botsch, Brack, Dietrich, Benedictus Ducis, Eckel, Eytelwein (5), Finck, Forster (9), Frosch, Fuchswild, Grefinger (5), Hofhaimer (11), Isaac, von Langenaw, Lapicida (7), Lemin (12), Machinger, St. Mahu, Peschin, Schonfelder, Senfl (8), Stoltzer (7), Uterholtzer, Wenck, Wolff (11), and 25 anonymous. This volume was reprinted several times, as follows:

Auszug guter alter und newer teutscher Liedlein einer rechten teutschen Art zu singen und auff allerley Instrumenten zubrauchen ... (Nürnberg: J. Petreius, 1543). Copy in CH:Bu.

Ein aussbund schöner teutscher Liedlein, zu singen, und auff allerley Instrument zu gebrauchen ... (Nürnberg: J. von Berg & U. Neuber, 1549). Copies in CH:Zz, BRD:B, and GB:Lbm.

Ein Aussbund schöner teutscher Liedlein, zu singen, und auff allerley Instrument, zugebrauchen ... (Nürnberg: J. von Berg & U. Neuber, 1552). Copies in BRD:As and Usche.

Ein Aussbund schöner teutscher Liedlein- zu singen, und auff allerley Instrument, zugebrauchen ... (Nürnberg: J. von Berg & U. Neuber, 1560). Copies in BRD:Mbs and DDR: ROu.

Selectissimae necnon familiarissimae cantiones, ultra centum vario idiomate vocum, tam multiplicium quam etiam paucar ... Besonder ausserlessner kunstlicher lustiger Gesanng mancherlay Sprachen ... von acht Stymmen an bis auf zwo: ... sinngen und auf Instrument zubrauchen (Augsburg: M. Kriesstein, 1540). Copy in A:Wn. The print contains 105 compositions by Arcadelt, Arthopius, Balduin, Barbe, Benedictus (8), Benoist, Blackenmüller, Brätel, Conseil, Courtois (6), Danckerts, Dietrich, Fevin, Frosch, Gardane, Gero, Gombert, Heugel, Isaac, Janequin, Jacquet, Jhan, Josquin (8), de La Rue, Lemlin, Lebrun, Lupi, S. Mahu, Mathias, Mouton, Peletier, Peschin, Regiensis, Richafort, Senfl (13), Sermisy, Susato, de Silva, Unterholtzer, Vinders, Verbonet, Verdelot, Willaert, and anonymous.

Hundert und fünfftzehen guter newer Liedlein, mit vier, fünff, sechs Stimmen vor nie im Truck auszgangen, deutsch, frantzösisch, welsch und lateinisch, lustig zu singen, und auff die Instrument dienstlich ... (Nürnberg: J. Ott, 1544). Copies in BRD:B and GB:Lbm. The print contains works by von Bruck, Breitengraser, Bruyer, Crecquillon, Dietrich, Eckel, Gombert, Hellinck, Isaac (10), Mahu, Morales, Müller, [Naich], Paminger, Reytter, Richafort, Senfl (64), de Silva, Stoltzer, Verdelot, Wannenmacher, and anonymous.

Der dritte Teyl, schöner, lieblicher, alter, und newe teutscher Liedlein nicht allein zu singen sonder auch auff allerley Instrumenten zu brauchen sehr dienstlich ... (Nürnberg: J. vom Berg & U. Neuber, 1549). Copy in BRD:B. The print contains 80 works by Blanckmüller, von Brant (10), Forster (20), von Langenaw, Lemlin, Müller, Othmayr (20), Senfl (7), Zyrler (9), and 8 anonymous.

Der dritte Teyl schöner, lieblicher, teutscher, Liedlein, nicht allein zu singen, sonder auch auff allerley Instrumenten zu brauchen ... (Nürnberg: J. vom Berg & U. Neuber, 1552). A slightly different collection than the above, copy in BRD:As. Reprinted as follows:

Der dritte Teyl schöner, lieblicher, teutscher Liedlein, nicht allein zu singen, sonder auch auff allerley Instrumenten zu brauchen ... (Nürnberg, J. vom Berg & U. Neuber, 1563). Copies in BRD:Mbs and DDR:ROu.

Etlicher gutter teutscher und polnicher Tentz biss in die anderthalbhundert mit fünff und vier Stimmen zugebrauchen auff allerley Instrument ... (Breslau: C. Scharffenberg, 1555, in five part-books). Copy in BRD:As (incomplete, S is missing).

Viel feiner lieblicher Stucklein spanischer welscher englischer frantzösischer Composition und Tentz uber drey hundert mit sechsen fünffen und vieren auff alle Instrument dienstlich mit sonderm Fleis ... (Breslau: C. Scharffenberg, 1555, in five part-books). Copy in BRD:As (incomplete, S is missing).

Der vierdt Theyl schöner frölicher frischer alter und newer teutscher Liedlein mit vier Stimmen nicht allein zu singen, sonder auch auff allen Instrumenten zu brauchen ... (Nürnberg: [J. vom Berg und U. Neuber], 1556, in four part-books). Copies in BRD:Mbs and DDR:ROu. The print contains 40 works by Blanckmüller, von Brant (15), Forster, Kilian, Othmayr, Pesch, Senfl (9), Zyrler (10), and anonymous.

Der fünffte Theil schöner frölicher frischer alter und newer teutscher Liedlein mit fünff Stimmen nicht allein zu singen, sonder auch auff allen Instrumenten zu brauchen bequem unnd ausserlesen (Nürnberg: J. von Berg & U. Neuber, 1556, in five part-books). Copies in BRD:Mbs and DDR:ROu. The print contains 52 compositions by von Bruck, Bauldouyn, von Brant (26), Crecquillon, Forster, Mahu, Matthias, Othmayr, Paminger, Pesch, Senfl (11), Stahel, and Willaert.

Schöner ausserlessner deutscher Psalm, und anderer künstlicher Moteten und geistlichen Lieder XX ... gantz lieblich zu singen, auch auff allerley Instrumenten, fast artlich und lustig zu gebrauchen ... (Nürnberg: U. Neuber, 1568, in four part-books). Copies in BRD:HB, KI, and Mbs. The print contains 20 works by Bischoff [Hagius], Docis, Otbmayr, Rabe, Schlegel, Selneccer, and 12 anonymous.

Schöner, ausserlessner, geistlicher und weltliche teutscher Lieder XX ... gantz lieblich zu singen, und auff allerley Instrumenten artlich und lustig zugebrauchen ... (München: A. Berg, 1585, in four part-books). Copies in BRD:Kl (incomplete, SAB only) and GB:Lbm (incomplete, T only). The print contains 20 works by Aichinger, Donato, Lechner, Le Febure, Meldaert, Scandelli, Schram, Walther, Utendal, and anonymous.

Teutsche Psalmen: geistliche Psalmen. mit dreyen Stimmen ... lieblich zu singen, sonder auch auff aller hand Art Instrumenten zugebrauchen. Durch Orlandum de Lasso, ... und seinen Sohn Rudolphum newlich componiert ... (München, A. Berg, 1588, in four part-books). Copy in BRD:PA.

Burck, Joachim

Zwantzig deutsche Liedlein mit vier Stimmen ... lieblich zu singen und auff Instrumenten zugebrauchen (Erfurt: Georg Baumann, 1575). Copies in BRD:As, B, and HB.

Vom Heiligen Ehstande: Viertzig Liedlein ... mit vier Stimmen lieblicher art zusingen, auch auff Instrumenten zugebrauchen (Leipzig: Jakob Apel and Mühlhausen: Georg Hantzsch, 1583, in four part-books). Copy in BRD:Mbs (incomplete ATB only S is missing). This work was reprinted as follows:

Vom Heiligen ... libri primi, zum andem Mahl gedruckt (Mühlhausen: Andreas Hantzsch, 1595). Copy in BRD:B.

Vom Heiligen ... libri secundi [sic], zum ersten mahl gedruckt (Mühlhausen: Andreas Hantzsch, 1596). Copy in BRD:B.

Demantius, Johannes Christoph

Neue Teutsche Weltiche Lieder, mit fünff Stimmen, welche nicht allein zu singen, sondern auch auff allerley Instrumenten zugebrauchen, gantz lieblich (Breslau: Andreas Wolcken and Nürnberg: Paul Kauffmann, 1595, in five part-books). Copy in BRD:Gs

Tympanum militare, Ungerische Heerdrummel und Feldgeschrey ... wie solche mit menschlicher Stimme, neben allerhand Instrument en, und Seitenspielen konnen musiciret und gesungen werden ... (Nürnberg: Katharina Dietrich, 1600, in six part-books). Copy in DDR:Dlb.

Sieben und siebentzig, neue ausserlesene, liebliche, zierliche, polnischer und teutscher Art, Täntze mit und ohne Texten, zu 4. und 5. Stimmen, neben andem künstlichen Galliarden, mit fünff Stimmen ... zu menschlicher Stimme, und allerley Instrumenten accommodiret (Nürnberg: Conrad Bauer [Katharina Dietrich], 1601, in five part-books). Copy in BRD:Hs. A modern edition of fifteen of these dances is avilable from London Pro Musica.

Dressler, Gallus

Ausserlesene teutsche Lieder, mit vier und fünff Stimmen, gantz lieblich zu singen, und auff allerley Instrumenten zugebrauchen (Nürnberg: Dietrich Gerlach, Wolfgang Kirchner, 1575, in five part-books). Copies in BRD:Kl and PL:WRu. This work was reprinted as follows:

Ausserlesene teutsche Lieder ... (Nürnberg: Katharina Gerlach & Johann Berg's Erben: Wolfgang Kirchner, 1580). Copies in BRD:Mbs and W.

Glanner, Caspar

Der Erste Theil, Neuer Teutscher Geistlicher und Weltlicher Liedlein, mit vier und fünff stimmen, welche nit allein lieblich zu singen, sonder auch auff allerley Instrumenten zu gebrauchen (München: Adam Berg, 1578, in four part-books). Copies in BRD:Mbs and PL:WRu.

Der Ander Theil, Neuer Teutscher Geistlicher und Weltlicher Liedlein, mit vier stimmen, welche nit allein lieblich zu singen, sonder auch auff allerley Instrumnten zu gebrauchen (München: Adam Berg, 1580, in four part-books). Copy in BRD:Mbs.

Harelbecanus, Sigerus Paulus

Psalmodia Davidica Des H. Proph. Davids verteutschte Psalmen mit fünff auch mehr und weniger Stimmen also zugericht, das man sie nicht allein singen, sondern auch auff allerley Instrumenten brauchen kan (Köln: Gerwinus Calenius, and: Johann Quentels Erban, 1590, in part-books). Copy in BRD:B (incomplete: A, T, and 5 only).

Harnisch, Otto Siegfried

Neue kurtzweilige Teutsche Liedtlein, Zu dreyen stimmen, welche gantz Lieblich zu singen und auff Instrumenten Zugebrauchen ... (Helmstedt: Jacob Lucius, 1587, in three part-books). Copy in BRD:Mbs.

Neue Auserlesene Teutsche Lieder, zu fünff und vier Stimmen, gantz lieblich zu singen, und auff Instrumenten zugebrauchen (Helmstedt: Jacob Lucius, 1588 in five part-books). Copies in BRD:Hs (incomplete: A, T, B, 5 only) and PL:WRu (incomplete: S, T, B only).

Neue lustige Teudsche Liedlein mit dreyen Stimmen...welche nicht allein lieblich zu singen sondern auch auff Musicalischen Instrumenten zu gebrauchen ... (Helmstedt: Lüdeken Brandt [Jacob Lucius], 1591, in part-books). No known copies survive.

Haussmann, Valentin

Neue Teutsche Weltliche Lieder, mit fünff stimmen, welchen am ende zwey mit sechsen hinzu gesetzt, lieblich zu singen, und auff Instrumenten wol zu gebrauchen

(Breslau: Andreas Wolcken and Nürnberg: Catharina Gerlachs Erben, 1592, in five part-books). Copy in PL:WRu.

Neue Teutsche weltliche Canzonette, mit 4 Stimmen, lieblich zu singen, und auff Instrumenten zugebrauchen (Nürnberg: Paul Kauffmann, 1596, in four part-books). Copy in PL:WRu.

Neue Teutsche Weltliche Lieder zu fünff Stimmen, mit höfelichen kurtzweiligen Texten, lieblich zu singen, und auff Instrumenten zugebrauchen (Nürnberg: Paul Kauffmann, 1597, in five part-books). Copies in GB:Lbm (incomplete: S, A, 5 only, T and B missing) and BRD:Ngm (incomplete: T only).

Neue artige und liebliche Täntze, zum theil mit Texten, das man kan mit Menschlicher Stimme zu Instrumenten singen, zum theil ohne Text gesetzt ... (Nürnberg: Paulum Kauffmann, 1598, in four part-books). This publication consisted of 21 dances fully texted and 25 without text (the latter included 10 pairs of dances, [Tantz] and 'Nach Tantz,' and 15 single dances. An incomplete copy was in DDR:Bds prior to the last war; its present status is unknown. The work was reprinted in 1599 for which incomplete copies exist in DDR:Bds (B only) and BRD:Hs (S, T, and 5 only; missing A and B).

Neue liebliche Melodien unter neue Teutsche Weltlich Texte, derer jeder einen besondern Namen anzeiget, mit vier Stimmen, dess mehrern theils zum Tantze zugebrauchen (Nürnberg: Paul Kauffmann, 1600 in four part-books). The first edition has not survived, but a fifth edition (1606) can be found in BRD:W and PL:WRu (here S and T in the original print and A and B in a manuscript copy).

Ausszug Auss ... zweyen unterschiedlichen Wercken, als der Teutschen Tantz mit 4. Stimmen und des Ersten Theils Polnischer Tantz, so Venus-Garten titulirt, mit 5. Stimmen, mit und ohne Text (Nürnberg: Paul Kauffmann [Balthasar Scherff], 1608, in part-books). Copy in BRD:B (incomplete: A only). This work was reprinted in 1609, a complete copy for which can be found in BRD:Usch. Twenty-five of these four-part dances can be found in a modern editon by London Pro Musica.

Hessen, Paul and Bartholomeus

Etlicher gutter Teutscher und Polnischer Tentz biss in die anderthalbhundert mit fünff und vier Stimmen, zugebrauchen. auff allerley Instrument dienstlich ... (Breslau: C. Scharffenberg, 1555, in five part-books). This publication consisted of 155 instrumental works without title or text. No complete copy exists, the most complete example is in BRD:As (missing the upper voice).

Viel feiner lieblicher Stucklein Spanischer Welscher, Englischer Frantzösischer composition und Tentz ... auff alle Instrument dieustlich (Breslau: C. Scharffenberg, 1555, in five part-books). No complete copy exists, the most complete example is in BRD:As (A, T, B, 5/6; missing S).

Hollander, Christiaan Jansz.

Neue Teutsche Geistliche und Weltliche Liedlein, mit viern, fünff, sechs, siben und acht stimmen, wölche gantz lieblich zusingen und auff allerley Instrumenten zugebrauchen ... (München: Adam Berg, 1570, in six part-books). No complete copies exist, those in both BRD:Mbs and DDR:ROu are missing the upper part.

Neue Ausserlesene Teutsche Lieder, mit vier, fünff und mehr Stimmen, welche gantz lieblich zu singen und auff allerley Instrumenten zugebrauchen (Nürnberg: Dieterich Gerlach, 1574, in six part-books). Copies in BRD:Kl and PL:WRu. A second edition (1575) can be found in BRD:Mbs.

Kugelmann, Paul

Etliche Teutsche Liedlein, Geistlich und Weltlich, mit Drey, Vier, Fünff unnd Sechs stimmen, auff alle Instrument zugebrauchen (Königsberg: Johann Daubmann 1558–1560, in part-books). Copy in PL:Tm.

Langius, Gregor

Neuer Deutscher Lieder mit dreyen Stimmen, welche nicht allein lieblich zu singen sondern auch auff allerley Instrumenten zu gebrauchen (Breslau: Johann Scharffenberg, 1584, in three part-books). Copy in BRD:Mbs. This work was reprinted in 1588, 1592, and 1598, for which no complete examples exist.

Der Ander Theirl Neuer Deudscher Lieder mit dreyen Stimmen, welche nicht allein lieblich zu singen sondern auch auff allerley Instrument en zu gebrauchen (Breslau: Andreas Wolcken [Johann Scharffenberg]), 1586, in three part-books). No complete examples exist for this edition or the following one (1590), but a complete copy of the third edition (1597) can be found in BRD:Hs.

Gregorii Langii ... Neugezierete Tricinia, lieblich zu singen und auff allerley Instrumenten zu gebrauchen ... (Erfurt: Martin Wittel, 1615, in three part-books). Copy in BRD:Hs.

Lechner, Leonhard

Neue Teutsche Lieder, mit Vier und Fünff Stimmen, Welche gantz lieblich zusingen, auch auff allerley Instrumenten zugebrauchen (Nürnberg: Nicolaus Knorr, 1577, in five part-books). Copies in BRD:Mbs, DDR:Bds, and GB:Lbm.

Lindner, Friderich

LIBER SECUNDUS GEMMAE MUSICALIS ... (Noribergae [Nürnberg]: Catharinae Gerlachiae, 1589). This publication contains 1 instrumental composition, in four parts, entitled, '*Fantasia Capriccio.*' Copies in BRD:As, Hs, Mbs, and Rp; DDR:Dl and Z; PL:GD; and S:Uu.

Lutkeman, Paul

Der Erst Theil. Newer Lateinishcer und deutsche Gesenge nebenst nachfolgenden schönen Fantasien, Paduanen und Galliaden lustig zusingen unnd gar lieblich auff allerley art Instrumenten zu gebrauchen, mit 5. 6. und mehr Stimmen Componiert ... (Stettin: Andree Kellnern Erben, 1597, in six part-books). All the compositions in this publication are by Lutkemann, ca. 1555–after 1611, who was a Stadtpfeifer at Wismar in 1578 and became chief Stadtpfeifer at Stettin from 1588 until ca. 1604. The first 28 compositions are for voices, the next 23 for instrumental ensemble in five parts, and the final 9 works are for instrumental ensemble in six parts. No complete copies are known to exist, BRD:W has five parts, the sixth is missing. A modern edition of the fourth fantasia, '*Innsbruck, ich muss dich lassen*,' is available from London Pro Musica.

[G1v]	*Fantasia*
[G2]	*Fantasia*
[G2v]	*Fantasia*
[G3]	*Fantasia, Isspruch ich muss dich:*
[G3v]	*Fantasia*
[G3v]	*Fantasia, Ich ruff zu dire*
[G4]	*Fantasia*
[H1]	*Fantasia*
[H1v]	*Fantasia, Er setz.*
[H2]	*Paduan*
[H2v]	*Galliard*
[H2v]	*Galliard*
[H3]	*Paduan*
[H3]	*Galliard*
[H3v]	*Fantasia*
[H4]	*Galliard*
[H4v]	*Paduan*
[I1]	*Paduan, Ohn dich muss:*
[I1]	*Galliard*
[I1v]	*Paduan*
[I1v]	*Galliard*
[I2]	*Galliard*
[I2]	*Galliard, Offt wünsch ich ihr.*

[I2v]   *Fantasia*
[I3]   *Galliard*
[I3v]   *Paduan*
[I3v]   *Galliard*
[I4]   *Paduan*
[I4v]   *Galliard*
[I4v]   *Galliard*
[K1]   *Fantasia*
[K1v]   *Galliard*

Le Maistre (Meistre, Maystre), Mattheus

Schöne und auserlesene Deudsche und Lateinische Geistliche Gesenge, Auff drey Stimmen ... zu singen und auff allerley Instrumenten zugebrauchen (Dresden: [Gimel Bergen] 1577, in three part-books). Copy in DDR:Z.

Mancinus, Thomas

Das Erste Buch Newer Lustiger, und Höfflicher Weltlicher Lieder ... (Helmstadt: Jacobum Lucium, 1588, in five part-books). This collection of vocal music also contains 1 instrumental work in four parts. Copy in BRD:Mbs.

Meiland, Jakob

Newe ausserlesene Teutsche Liedlin, mit fünff und vier Stimmen, so beide zusingen und auch auff allerley Instrument en zugebrauchen (Nürnberg: Dietrich Gerlach, 1569, in five part-books). Copies in BRD:HB and DDR:Z.

Neuwe ausserlesene Teutsche Gesang, mit vier und fünff stimmen, so gantz lieblich zu singen und auff allerley Instrument zu gebrauchen (Frankfurt: Georg Corvinus & Sigmund Feyerabend, 1575, in five part-books). Copies in BRD:HB, Mbs; DDR:Dl; PL:WRu; and S:Uu.

Otto, Georg

Geistliche deutsche Gesenge D. Martini Lutheri. 1588. Auff die fürnembste Feste und sonsten zu singen, Auch allerley Instrumenten zu gebrauchen, mit Fünff und Sechs Stimmen componiret (Erfurt: Georg Baumann, 1588, in five part-books). Copy in BRD:Mbs.

Praetorius, Abraham

Neue Geistliche Teutsche des Koniglichen Propheten Davidis Psalmen gantz lieblich zu singen und auff allerley Instrumenten zu gebrauchen, mit fünff Stimmen componirt (Greifswald: Augustin Ferber, 1592, in five part-books). Copies in DDR:SWl and ROu.

Praetorius, Christoph

Fröliche und liebliche Ehrnlieder, von züchtiger Lieb und Ebelicher treu auff ein sondere Art zu singen und auff Instrumenten zugebrauchen, mit vier stimmen gemacht (Wittenberg: Matthias Welack, 1581, in four part-books). Copy in BRD:Mbs.

Der ander Teil. Frölicher und lieblicher Ehrnlieder ... zu singen und auff Instrumenten zugebrauchen, mit vier stimmen gemacht (Wittenberg: Matthias Welack, 1581, in four part-books). Copy in BRD:Mbs.

Regnart, Jacob

Neue Kurtzweilige Teutsche Lieder mit fünff stimmen, welche gantz lieblich zu singen, und auff allerley Instrumenten zugebrauchen (Nürnberg: Katharina Gerlach & Johann Bergs Erben, 1580, in five part-books). Copies in BRD:B, Hs, Mbs, Usch, and GB:Lbm. This work was reprinted in 1586, copies in BRD:B; PL:GD, Tü; and US:Wc.

Kurtzweilige neue Teutsche Lieder mit vier Stimmen welche gantz lieblich zusingen und auff allerley Instrumenten zugebrauchen (München: Adam Berg, 1591, in four part-books). Copy in BRD:Mbs (incomplete: S only).

Threni amorum. Der ander Theil Lustiger weltlicher lieder mit fünff stimmen ... nicht allein auff allerley Instrumenten sonder auch mit menschlicher stimm gar zierlich und ahnmütig zugebrauchen (Nürnberg: Paul Kauffmann, 1595). Only incomplete copies are extant, in BRD:B (S,A,T, and 5 only), GB:Lbm (A only), and S:Uu (T only).

Scandello, Antonio

Neue Teutsche Liedlein mit Vier und Fünff Stimmen, welche gantz lieblich zu singen und auff allerley Instrument en zugebrauchen (Nürnberg, Dietrich Gerlach, 1568, in five part-books). Copies in BRD:HB, Mbs, and W, all incomplete containing only S,A,T,B. The remaining part can be found only in BRD:Kl.

Nawe und lustige Weltliche Deudsche Liedlein mit Vier, fünff und Sechs Stimmen auff allerley Instrumenten zugebrauchen und lieblich zu singen (Dresden: Matthes Stöckel & Gimel Bergen, 1570, in five part-books). Copy in BRD:Gs. A later edition appeared in 1578, for which no complete examples survive.

Nawe schöne ausseresene Geistliche Deudsche Lieder mit Fünff und Sechs Stimmen, gantz lieblich zu singen, Und auff allerley Instrumenten zugebrauchen, Sampt einem Dialogo mit Acht Stimmen (Dresden: Gimel Bergen, 1575, in five part-books). Copies in BRD:Kl and DDR:Dl.

Schöne Weltliche und Geistliche Nawe Deudsche Liedlein mit Vier, Fünff und Sechs Stimmen auff allerley Instrumenten zugebrauchen und lieblich zu singen (Dresden: Gimel Bergen, 1579, in part-books). No complete examples are extant, only the tenor survives in BRD:LÜh, DDR:Dl, and PL:WRu.

Schramm, Melchior

Neue ausserlesene Teutsche Gesang, ... mit vier Stimmen, welche gantz lieblich zu singen und auff allerley Instrument zu gebrauchen (Frankfurt: Sigmund Feyerabend [Georg Raben], 1579, in four part-books). Copies in BRD:Mbs and DK:Kk.

Syringus, Jacobus

Cantiones poenitentiales. Christliche neue Teutsche Gesänge ... mit Fünff stimmen gantz lustig zu singen und auff allerley Instrumenten zu gebrauchen ... (Ülzen: Michael Kroner, 1582, in five part-books). No complete copies are extant, although for a second edition (1588) one copy exists in BRD:Kl.

Utendal (Utenthal, Uttendal), Alexander

Fröliche neue Teutsche unnd Frantzösische Lieder lieblich zu singen auch auff allerley Instrumenten zugebrauchen nach sonderer art der Music Componirt mit vier fünff und mehr stimmen (Nürnberg: Dietrich Gerlach, 1574, in five part-books). Copies in BRD:Hs, Mbs, Nla, and S:V. There are no extant complete copies for the second edition of 1586.

Wend, Johann

Der Erste Theil Neuer Teutscher Geistlicher Lieder ... Mit 3 Stimmen zu singen und auff allerley Instrumenten zu gebrauchen componirt (Hamburg Philipp von Ohr, 1597, in three part-books). Copy in BRD:Hs.

Der Ander Theil Neuer Teutscher Geistlicher Lieder ... (Hamburg Philipp von Ohr, 1597, in three part-books). Copy in BRD:Hs.

Print Collections Without Instrument Designation

Becker, Carl

Die Hausmusik in Deutschland in dem 16, 17, 18 Jahrhunderts (Leipzig: 1840). This edition, for keyboard, includes transcriptions of three dances of the sixteenth century: '*Deutscher Tanz*' (1571), '*Herzog Moritz Tanz*' (1571), and '*Englischer Tanz*' (1577), without sources. Copy in F:Pn (40.B.5).

Agricola, Martin

DUO LIBRI MUSICES, CONTINENTES COMpendium artis , & illustria exempla ... (Wittenberg: Georg Rhau 1561). This is a music theory text with 54 textless compositions in three and four parts presented in connection with instrumental instruction. Copies in BRD:B, HB, and HVl. A modern edition exists by H. Funck, ed., *Instrumentalische Gesange um 1545* (Wolfenbüttel, 1933).

Kugelmann, Johann

Concentus novi, trium vocum, ecclesiarum usui in Prussia praecipue accomodati. Joanne Kugelmanno, tubicinae symphoniarum authore ... (Augsburg: M. Kriesstein [ca. 1540]). This collection by a court trumpeter contains 39 works in four, five, six, and eight parts, by Blanckenmüller, Heugel, Kugelmann (30), Schnellinger, Stoltzer, and 3 anonymous. Copies in A:Wn and BRD:Mbs.

Single Title Manuscripts Designated for Winds

Anonymous

[4] *Sonate*, for 'Bombardi.' BRD:Kl (under '12 Sonate f. Gambe,' Kat. S.62).

Cornazzani, Phileno Agostino (ca. 1543–1628)

'Piece for four choirs' [lost], in which trumpets were used 'so Zuvor unerhört, eleganti harmonia.' Cornazzani was a trombonist in the court band of Emperor Ferdinand I, ca. 1552 – ca.1564, and later served in the courts at Graz and Munich.

Heugel, Johannes (1500–1585)

'*Lerman*,' according to Grove,[3] this is an unusual instrumental work specifically composed for wind instruments. BRD:Kl.

[3] Grove, 8:540.

Kugelmann, Paul (d. 1580)

Laudate Dominum, 1541, a vocal canon accompanied by four zinks and four trombones. Kugelmann, brother to Johann Kugelmann, was a court trumpeter in Königsberg, ca. 1542–1580. DK:Kk (Gl.Kgl.Saml. 1872).

Lasso, Orlando (1532–1594)

Tenebrae factae sunt, for SATB, three trombones and organ. This copy, ca. 1820, represents a work which apparently is not in the Lasso GA. BRD:WS (MS. 468).

Senfl

'Ich klag den tag,' according to Grove[4] the work has a bass, 'auff Posaun und Krumhorn.'

[4] Grove, 5:74, no source given.

Stolzer, Thomas

Erzurne dich nicht, 1526, in six-parts, which the composer recommended could be played by an ensemble of crumhorns, 'since it suits them throughout, which is not the case with every composition, especially those in many parts.'[5] Copy in DDR:Z (CVI, 5).

[5] Quoted in Gustave Reese, *Music in the Renaissance* (New York: Norton, 1954), 725.

Walther, Johann (1496–1570)

[26] *Fugen*, composed, 'especially for cornetts,' by Luther's musical advisor. Copy in DDR: LEu (MS. Cod. Mus. 50, 'Thomaskirche'). These works are reprinted in a modern edition in *Johann Walter Sämtliche Werke* (Kassel, 1973), 4:77–120.

SINGLE TITLE MANUSCRIPTS WITHOUT INSTRUMENT DESIGNATION

Anonymous

Canzon, in ten parts, 'in Echo.' BRD:Kl (MS. fol. 59r).

Herwich, Chr.

[61] *Pavenen*, in five parts, and *Gagliarden*, in four parts. BRD:Kl.

Lechner, Leonhard

Pavana Lachrymae, in four parts. DDR:Bds.

SINGLE TITLE PRINTS DESIGNATED FOR WINDS

Lasso

Motette, performed by five zinks and two trombones. The work is contained in M. Troiano, *Dialoghi* (Venice, 1569).

SINGLE TITLE PRINTS WITHOUT INSTRUMENT DESIGNATION

Aicbinger, Gregor (1564–1628)

Liber II. *Sacarum Cantionum* (Venice: 1595), contains 3 ricercari in four parts. BRD:Kl

[36] *Ricercar Primi Toni*
[38] *Ricercar per sonare & cantare*
[40] *Ricercar per sonare & cantare*

Biffi, Gioseffo

Il primo libro delle canzonette a sei voci per cantar & sonare, insieme con alcune latine, una todesca, & una battaglia (Nürnberg: Paul Kauffmann, 1596, in six part-books). No complete copies survive. BRD:F (S, 5, and 6 only) and W (T only).

HUNGARY

Manuscript Collections Without Instrument Designation

H:Bn (MS. Bártfa Mus. Pro 9 [a-e]), ca. 1542, five part-books, contains 1 textless composition.

H:Bn (MS. Bártfa Mus. Pro 6 [a-d]), after 1558, four part-books, contains 3 textless hymns and an additional textless polyphonic composition.

H:Bn (MS. Bártfa 31), ca. 1570–1650, contains 1 incomplete textless polyphonic composition.

ITALY

Manuscript Collections Without Instrument Designation

I:Rc (MS. 2856), sixteenth century, contains three- and four-part works with text incipits in all voices.

I:Rvat (MS. Cappella Giulia, Cod. XIII, 27), sixteenth century, prepared for Leo x, contains three-part works with text or incipit in one voice and textless in the remaining two.

I:Fn (MS. Magl. XIX, 178), sixteenth century, contains three-part works with an incipit in one voice and textless in the remaining two, three-part works with incipits in all voices, and four-part works with incipits in one voice and textless in the remaining three.

I:Fn (MS. Magl. XIX, 176), sixteenth century, contains three-part compositions with incipits in all voices.

I:Fn (MS. Magl. XIX, 121), sixteenth century, contains three-part works with incipits in one voice and textless in the remaining two.

I:Fc (MS. Basevi 2439), sixteenth century, contains four-part compositions with text in one voice and incipits in the remaining three.

I:Fn (MS. Panciatichi 27), early sixteenth century, Northern Italy, contains 6 polyphonic textless works, including an anonymous 'caminata' in four-parts with passamezzo antico-like harmonies.

I:Mt (MS. 55), early sixteenth century, Northern Italy, perhaps Milan, contains 5 polyphonic textless compositions.

I:VEcap (MS. DCCLVII), early sixteenth century, Northern Italy, contains more than 60 textless compositions in three to five parts.

I:TRc (MS. 1947–4), early sixteenth century, contains German songs and chansons without text.

I:Mcap(d) (MS. Librone 4), early sixteenth century, compiled for the Milan Cathedral, contains 1 polyphonic textless composition.

I:Tn (MS. Riserva Musicale I. 27), ca. 1500, Turin, contains 1 textless French secular work.

GB:Lbm (MS. Egerton 3051), ca. 1500, Northern Italy, perhaps Florence, contains 53 works, some without text and some with incipits only.

F:Pn (MS. Rés. Vm 7.676), 1502, Mantua, for the court of Isabella d'Este or Ferrara, for the court of Ercole 1 d'Este, contains 2 polyphonic textless compositions.

I:Fn (MS. Magl. XIX. 117), ca. 1505–1520 in France, with additions ca. 1510–1521, Florence. The manuscript contains 11 polyphonic textless compositions.

I:PEc (MS. 1013 [M.36]), 1509, Venice, contains 61 textless compositions, which include 7 Mass Ordinary sections, 4 Mass Proper sections, 4 motets, 8 French secular pieces, and 3 Italian secular pieces.

I:Fn (MS. Magl. XIX 107 bis), ca. 1510–1513, contains four-part works with an incipit in one voice and textless in the remaining three voices.

I:Fn (MS. II.I.232), ca. 1515, Florence, contains 1 textless motet.

I:Fc (MS. Basevi 2440), ca. 1515–1520, Florence, contains 2 polyphonic textless works.

I:Bc (MS. R. 142), ca. 1515–1530, Northern Italy, contains 1 polyphonic textless composition.

I:Bc (MS. Q. 19), 1518, contains four-part works with incipits in all voices.

I:Fn (MS. Banco Rari 337), ca. 1520, probably Florence, contains 49 polyphonic textless compositions.

I:CMbc (MS. D [F]), ca. 1521–1526, Casale Monferrato, contains 2 polyphonic textless compositions.

I:Bc (MS. Q. 21), ca. 1523–1527, Florence, contains 1 polyphonic textless composition.

I:MOd (MS. IV), ca. 1520–1530, compiled for the Modena Cathedral, contains 2 textless canons.

I:MOd (MS. XI), ca. 1520–1530, compiled for the Modena Cathedral, contains 1 polyphonic textless work.

I:Rvat (MS. Vaticani Musicali 571), ca. 1520–1540, contains 1 polyphonic textless work.

I:Fn (MS. Magl. XIX 99–102), ca. 1540 or later, Florence, in four part-books, contains several instrumental compositions.

I:BGi (MS. 1209 D), ca. 1545, contains 1 polyphonic textless composition.

I:Bc (MS. Q. 22), ca. 1550, in four part-books, contains 3 polyphonic textless works.

GB:Lbm (MS. Roy. App. 59–62), ca. 1550–1560, in four part-books, contains 44 dances.

I:Fn (MS. Magl. XIX 107), second-half, sixteenth century,
a score containing 23 ricercares in four parts. Three are
anonymous, 10 are by Buus (from the 1547 print) and 10 are
by Malvezzi (from the 1577 print).

BRD:Usch (MS. 237 [a-d]), 1557, Lucca, in four part-books,
contains 6 polyphonic textless compositions.

I:VEcap (MS. MCXXVIII), ca. 1585, four of the original six
part-books, contain '*Canzone da suonare*,' as follows (folio
pages given):

Four Voice:
[6]   Crequition
[10]   Merulo
[11]   Merulo
[12]   Merulo
[20]   Merulo
[22]   Guami
[25]   Al Sfoi
[34]   Chabril
[1–5,7–9,12,16,17,18,19,23,26–33,35, and 36] are Anonymous

Five Voice:
[44–50] Anonymous

Six Voice:
[51–52] Anonymous

F: Pn (MS. Rés. Vma. 851), late sixteenth century, Parma
or Ravenna, contains 33 polyphonic instrumental compositions.

I:Bc (MS. Q. 35), 1603, Brescia, a score which contains 21 canzonas in four parts by Maschera.

Print Collections Designated for Winds

Banchieri, Adriano

CANZONI ALLA FRANCESE A QUATTRO VOCI
PER SONARE Dentrovi, un Echo, & in fine una
Battaglia a Otto, & dui Concerti … (Venetia: Ricciardo
Amadino, 1596). Copy in I:Bc. A modern edition of the

twelve canzonas is available from London Pro Musica. The original print contains four-part instrumental works as follows:

[1] Canzon Prima. *La Rovattina*
[2] Canzon seconda. *L'Ardina*
[3] Canzon Terza. *La Galluppa*
[4] Canzon Quarta. *La Rustica*
[5] Canzon Quinta. *La Pomponazza*
[6] Canzon Sesta. *L'Alcenagina*
[6] Canzon Settima. *La Guamina* (Gioseffo Guami)
[8] Canzon Ottava. *La Banchierina*
[9] Canzon Nona. *La Camerina*
[10] Canzon Decima. *La Feliciana*
[11] Canzon Undecima. *La Organistina Bella* ('In Echo')
[12] *La Battaglia* a8 ('Concerto primo … Udite ecco le trombe')
[14] *Magnificat* a8 ('Concerto secondo')
[16] *Suscepit Israel* ('Concerto terzo')

Dalla Casa, Girolamo

IL VERO MODO DI DIMINUIR, CON TUTIE LE SORT I DI STROMENTI Di fiato, & corda, & di voce Humana … (Venetia: Angelo Gardano, 1584). Copy in I:Bc. This is one of the most important early collections for wind ensemble, compiled by the director of the Venetian State Wind Ensemble and the most famous cornett player of the sixteenth century. It is generally taken to represent his original solo cornett parts, intended to be added to the pre-existant works listed. Thus it most probably represents the solo repertoire he performed while accompanied by his Venetian State Wind Ensemble. For modern performance, one takes the original music cited, transcribes it for wind ensemble, and then adds to it the original upper voice given here. The original works upon which he based the solo parts given here are:

[7] Io *canterei d'Amour*. Cipriano [da Rore] a4
[8] *Non e ch'el duol*. Cipriano a4
[9] *La bella netta ignuda & bianca mano*. Cipriano a4

[11]	*Signor mio caro.* Cipriano a4
[12]	*Carita di Signore.* Cipriano a4
[13]	*Nasce la pena mia.* Striggio a6
[14]	*I dolci colli.* Striggio a6
[14]	2a pars [*Et qual cervo ferito*]
[15]	*La prima vergine.* Cipriano a5
[15]	*Cantai un tempo.* Filippo de Monte a6
[16]	*La nona Vergine.* Cipriano a5
[16]	*Se la gratia divina.* Adriano [Willaert] a5
[16]	*La ver l'aurora.* Striggio a6
[17]	*La quarta vergine.* Cipriano a5
[18]	*La quinta vergine.* Cipriano a5
[19]	*Di tempo in tempo.* Cipriano a4
[20]	*Dall'estremo Orizonte.* Cipriano a5
[20]	*La sesta vergine.* Cipriano a5
[21]	*S'amor la viva fiamma.* Cipriano a5
[21]	*Dale belle contrade.* Cipriano a5
[22]	*Alla dolc'ombra.* Cipriano a4
[22]	3a pars [*Un lauro mi diffese*]
[22]	4a pars [*Però più ferm'ogn'hor*]
[23]	5a pars [*Selve, sassi, campagne*]
[23]	6a pars [*Tanto mi piacque*]
[23]	*La seconda vergine.* Cipriano a5
[24]	*La terza vergine.* Cipriano a5
[25]	*La seconda parte De quando fra l'altre donne.* Cipriano a5
[25]	*Dolce ritorn'amor.* Striggio a6
[27]	[*Il n'est plaisir*] Canzon a 6 di Martin Peu d'Argent
[29]	*Helas ma mere.* Adriano a5
[32]	*Si me tenez.* [Crecquillon] a6
[34]	*Rossignolet.* Clemens non Papa a4
[36]	*Voules ouiir.* Adriano a5
[39]	*Ancor ch'io possa dire.* Striggio a6
[40]	*Amor mi struggie il cor.* Andrea Gabrieli a6
[40]	*Ringratto & lodo il ciel.* Andrea Gabrieli a6
[41]	2a pars [*Amor rimanti in pace*]
[42]	*Alla fontaine.* Adriano a6
[44]	*Larose.* Gombert a6
[46]	*Di virtu di costumi.* Cipriano a5

IL VERO MODO DI DIMINUIR, CON TUTTE LE SORTE DI STROMENTI Di fiato, & corda, & di voce Humana … (Venetia: Angelo Gardano, 1584). Copy in I:Bc. This is the second volume of the Dalla Casa work described above. This volume contains some works for solo viola bastarda and lute, which are not listed here. In folio 38 he presents all voices of the work given, with ornamentation. The works listed are assumed to be for solo cornett and wind ensemble.

[1]   *Canzon delli Ucelli*. Clemens Janequin
[2]   2a pars [*Vous orrez*]
[3]   3a pars [*Rossignol*]
[4]   4a pars [*Arriere*]
[5]   *Frais & gaillart*. Clemens non Papa a4
[6]   *Frais & gaillart*. Alio modo
[7]   *Petite fleur coincte*. Tomas Crequillon a4
[8]   *Alix avoit*. Tomas Crequillon a4
[9]   *Petit Jacquet*. Curtois a4
[10] *Oncques amour*. Tomas Crequillon a5
[11] *Oncques amour*. Alio modo
[12] *Susana un giur*. Orlando Lasso a5
[13] *Susanna un giur*. Alio modo
[14] *Joyssance*. Adriano [Willaert] a5
[16] *Content*. Tomas Crequillon a4
[38] Alla dolc'ombra. Cipriano a4 ('*Canzon di Cipriano tutte le quattro parte diminuite*')
[40] 2a pars [*Non vidde'l mondo*]
[42] 3a pars [*Un lauro mi diffese*]
[44] 4a pars [*Pero piu ferm'ogn'hor*]
[46] 5a pars [*Selve sassi campagne*]
[48] 6a pars [*Tanto mi piacque*]

Gabrieli, Andrea, and Padovano, Annibale

DIALOGHI MUSICALI DE DIVERSI ECCELLENTIS-SIMI AUTORI, A Sette, Otto, Nove, Dieci, Undeci & Dodeci Voci … CON DUE BATTAGLIE A OTTO VOCI, Per sonar de Istrumenti da Fiato … (Venetia: Angelo Gardano, 1590, in twelve part-books). Copy in B:Br. This work was reprinted in 1592 and 1594, but no complete copies are extant of the later editions. A modern edition of the Padovano work can be found in *Istituzioni e Monumenti dell'Arte Musical Italiana* (Milano, 1931), 1:177–202.

[49] *Aria della Battaglia per sonar d'Istrumenti da fiato a8.* Annibale Padoano
[50] 2a pars
[52] *Aria della Battaglia per sonar d'Istrumenti da fiato a8.* Andrea
[53] 2a pars

Gabrieli, Giovanni

SACRAE SYMPHONIAE, JOANNIS GABRIELLI ... Senis, 7, 8, 10, 12, 14, 15, & 16 Tam vocibus, Quam Instrumentis ... (Venetiis: Angelum Gardanum, 1597, in twelve part-books). Copy in A:Wn. The canzonas in folios 33 and 34 were also printed (folios [I4v] and [K1]) by Paul Kaufmann, *FIORI DEL GIARDINO DI DIVERSI ECCELLENTISSIMI AUTORI ...* (NORIMBERGO [Nürnberg], 1597. Copies in BRD:DS and PL:GD. The SACRAE SYMPHONIAE print of 1597 contains works with Latin text and the following instrumental compositions. A modern edition of the instrumental works is available from Musica Rara.

[30] *Canzon Primi Toni* a8.
[31] *Canzon Septimi Toni* a8.
[32] *Canzon Septimi Toni* a8.
[33] *Canzon Noni Toni* a8.
[34] *Canzon Duodecimi Toni* a8.
[35] *Sonata Pian & Forte* a8. Alla Quarta Bassa (for cornetto, 6 trombones, and 'violino')
[44] *Canzon Primi Toni* a 10.
[45] *Canzon Duodecimi Toni* a10.
[46] *Canzon Duodecimi Toni* a10.
[47] *Canzon Duodecimi Toni* a10 (upper part is specified as cornetto)
[48] *Canzon in Echo Duodecimi Toni* a10. (for 8 cornetti and 2 trombones)

[49] *Canzon* sudetta accomodata per concertar con l'Organo a10. (for 8 cornetti and 2 trombones [no organ part exists])

[57] *Canzon Septimi* & Octavi Toni a12.

[58] *Canzon Noni Toni* a12.

[59] *Sonata Octavi Toni* a12.

[62] *Canzon Quarti Toni* a15. (for 2 cornetti, 'violino,' and 12 trombones)

SYMPHONIAE SACRAE II ... (Venezia: Gardano, 1615, in fifteen part-books). Copies in BRD:As (incomplete: B is missing) and GB:Ob (incomplete: library has A, B, and '13'). This print contains the following works for voices and winds.

[Nr. 15] *Jubilate Deo* a 10. (for 2 voices, 2 cornetti, 5 trombones, and bassoon [doubled by ad. Lib voice])

[Nr. 20] *Suscipe* a12. (for 6 voices and 6 trombones)

[Nr. 25] *Quem vidistis* a14. (for 6 voices, 2 cornetti, 3 trombones, and 3 unspecified instrumental parts)

Canzoni et Sonate per sonar con ogni sorte de instrumenti ... (Venezia: Gardano, 1615, in thirteen part-books). Copies in BRD:As (incomplete: missing B), I:Rsc (incomplete: library has A, T, B, and '5'), and DDR:Bds (was complete, but since the war the status is uncertain). A modern edition is available from Musica Rara.

Works specified for winds

[Nr. 18] *Sonata* a14. (for 4 cornetti and 10 trombones)

[Nr. 20] *Sonata* a22. (for 1 cornett, 2 trombones, and 19 unspecified parts)

Works without specific instrumentation

[Nr. 1] *Canzon* a5.

[Nr. 2] *Canzon* a6.

[Nr. 3] *Canzon* a6.

[Nr. 5] *Canzon* a7.

[Nr. 6] *Canzon* a7.

[Nr. 7] *Canzon* a7.

[Nr. 8] *Canzon* a8.

[Nr. 9] *Canzon* a8.

[Nr. 12] *Canzon* a8.

[Nr. 13] *Sonata* a8.
[Nr. 16] *Canzon* a12.
[Nr. 19] *Sonata* a15.

Ganassi, Silvestro di.

Opera Intitulata Fontegara Laquale insegna a sonare di flauto chon tutta l'arte opportuna a esso instrumento massime il diminuire il quale sara utile ad ogni instrumento di fiato et chorde ... (Venice, 1535, with a plate showing three men around a table playing recorders from part-books and one man singing). Copies in DDR:Bds and Ju; BRD:W (containing an appendix in Ganassi's hand with an additional 175 diminutions on one six-note figure!); Copies in I:Bc and Fc; and US:Wc. This publication contains no complete compositions, but numerous examples of written out improvisation.

PRINT COLLECTIONS DESIGNATED FOR ANY INSTRUMENT

Agostini, Lodovico

IL NUOVO ECHO A cinque voci DEL R.do MONS. or DON LODOVICO AGOSTINI FERRARESE ... (Ferrara, 1583, in five part-books). Copies in I:MOe and Tn. This print contains two five-part instrumental compositions.

[11] *FANTASIA* da Sonar con gli Istromenti. Ad imitatione del Sig. Alessandro Striggio
[13] INTRAMEZZO

Bassano, Giovanni

FANTASIE A TRE VOCl, PER CANTAR ET SONAR con ogni sorte d'Instrumenti ... (Venetia: Giacomo Vincenzi & Ricciardo Amadino, 1585, in three part-books). Copies in GB:Lbm (incomplete: B only) and DDR:Bds (since the war, status uncertain). Contains 20 fantasias in three-parts.

RICERATE PASSAGGI ET CADENTIE, Per potersi essercitar nel diminuir terminatamente con ogni sorte d'Instrumento … (Venetia: Giacomo Vincenzi & Ricciardo Amadino, 1585, in folios). Copy in I:Bc. Contains nine highly ornamented monophonic ricercares by Bassano (8) and Rore.

IL FIORE DE CAPRICI MUSICALI A QUATRO VOCI Per sonar con ogni sorte di stromenti … (Venetia, Giacomo Vincenzi, 1588, in four part-books). Copy in I:Bc (incomplete: T only). This publication contained 20 four-part compositions without titles.

Bendusi, Francesco

OPERA NOVA DE BALLI … Accommodati da cantare & sonare d'ogni sorte de Stromenti … (Venetia, Antonio Gardane, 1553, in four part-books). Copies in A:Wgm and BRD:Mbs. A modern edition is available from London Pro Musica. The original print contained 24 four-part compositions as follows.

[1] *Pass'e mezo dit to il Romano*
[1] *Moschetta*
[2] *Desiderata*
[2] *Pietoso*
[3] *Speranza*
[3] *La mala vecchia*
[4] *Il stocco*
[4] *Doi stanchi*
[5] *La falilela*
[5] *La Bruna*
[5] *E Dove vastu o bon solda*
[6] *Chi non ha martello*
[6] *Incognita*
[7] *Bella foresta*
[7] *Galante*
[8] *Fusta*
[8] *Animoso*
[8] *Cortesa Padoana*
[9] *Bandera*
[9] *Gioia*

[9] *La Giovenetta*
[10] *Il ben ti vegna*
[10] *Pass'e mezo ditto il Compasso*
[11] *Violla*

Mainerio, Giorgio

IL PRIMO LIBRO DE BALLI A QUATRO VOCI, ACCOMMODATI PER CANTAR ET SONAR D'OGNI Sorte de Istromenti ... (Venetia: Angelo Gardano, 1578, in four part-books). Copy in I:Tn. A modern edition by Helmut Monkemeyer was published by Edition Moeck, Nr. 3616.

[1] *La Billiarda*
[1] *Saltarello*
[2] *Pass'e mezzo antico in cinque modi*
[3] *Represa in tre modi*
[4] *Saltarello in quattro modi*
[4] *Represa*
[5] *Pass'e mezzo della Paganina*
[5] *Saltarello*
[6] *Caro Ortolano*
[6] *Saltarello*
[6] *Gagliarda*
[7] *Putta Nera Ballo Furlano*
[8] *La Zanetta Padoana*
[9] *La Saporita Padoana*
[10] *Todescha*
[10] *Saltarello*
[11] *La Lavandara Gagliarda*
[12] *Pass'e mezzo Moderno in cinque modi*
[13] *Represa in quattro modi*
[14] *Saltarello in tre modi*
[14] *Represa*
[14] *Scharazula Marazula*
[15] *Tedescha*
[15] *Saltarello*
[16] *Ungaresca*
[16] *Saltarello*
[17] *L'arboscello ballo Furlano*

[17] *Ballo Millanese*
[18] *La Parma*
[18] *Saltarello*
[19] *Ballo Francese in doi modi*
[19] *Saltarello*
[20] *Ballo Anglese*
[20] *Saltarello*
[21] *Todescha*
[21] *Saltarello*
[22] *La fiamenga*

Mazzi, Luigi

RICERCARI A QUATTRO ET CANZONI A QUATTRO, A CINQUE, ET A OTTO VOCI Da Cantare, & Sonare con ogni sorte d'Instrumenti … (Venetia: Giacomo Vincenti, 1596, in four part-books). Copy in I:Fn. This publication by the organist at San Benedetto in Ferrara contains 8 ricercars and 8 canzonas, all in four parts, the title to the contrary.

Vincenti, Giacomo (Publisher)

CANZON DI DIVERSI PER SONAR CON OGNI SORTE DI STROMENTI A quatro, Cinque, & Sei Voci … (Venetia: Giacomo Vincenzi, 1588, in six part-books). Copy in CH:Bu.

[1] *L'olica*. Claudio [Merulo] da Coreggio a4
[2] *Torna*. Crequilon a4
[2] Giosefo Guami a4
[4] Giosefo Guami a4
[5] *Las voules*. a5
[6] *On ques Amor*. a5
[7] *Viver ne puis*. A5
[8] *Io visans*. A5
[9] *Content*. A5
[10] *Sine tenez*. a6
[11] *Sire*. a6
[12] *A la fontaine*. a6
[13] *La rose*. a6

Print Collections Without Instrument Designation

Anonymous Compilers

Canzoni francese a due voci di Ant. Gardane, et di altri autori, buone da cantare et sonare … (Venezia: A. Gardane, 1539, in two part-books). Copies in A:Wn and I:PLn. Contains 28 compositions by Gardane (22), Le Heurteur, Peletier, and Sermisy.

Fantasie Recercari Contrapunti a tre voci … per cantare et sonare d'ogni sorte di stromenti … (Venezia: A. Gardano, 1551, in three part-books). Copy in I:Fm (incomplete, S only). A complete copy of a later edition (1559) can be found in BRD:Mbs. The original print contained 17 compositions by Barges, Jeronimo da Bologna, Rore, Willaert (10), and 2 anonymous.

Arrivabene, Andrea (Publisher)

MUSICA NOVA ACCOMMODATA PER CANTAR ET SONAR SOPRA ORGANI; ET ALTRI STRUMENTI … (1540, in four part-books). Copy in I:Bc (incomplete: B only).

[N2]	R[icercare] ADRIAN WILLAERT
[N2v]	R. JULIO DA MODENA
[N3]	R. JULIO DA MODENA
[N3v]	R. JULIO DA MODENA
[N4v]	R. JULIO DA MODENA
[O1]	R. JULIO DA MODENA
[O1v]	R. NICOLO BENOIST
[O2v]	R. JULIO DA MODENA
[O3]	R. JULIO DA MODENA
[O3v]	R. ADRIAN WILLAERT
[O4]	JULIO DA MODENA
[O4v]	R. JULIO DA MODENA
[P1]	R. JULIO DA MODENA
[P1v]	R. ADRIAN WILLAERT
[P2v]	R. JULIO DA MODENA
[P3v]	R. JULIO DA MODENA
[P4v]	R. GUILIELMO GOLIN
[Q2]	R. JULIO DA MODENA

[Q2v] R. JULIO DA MODENA
[Q3v] R. Hieronimo [Cavazzoni] da bologna
[Q4v] Da pacem. Bieronimo parabsco

Banchieri, Adriano

CONCERTI ECCLESIASTICI ... Aggiontovi nel Primo Choro la Spartitura per sonare nell'Organo commodissima ... (Venetia: Giacomo Vencenti, 1595, in nine part-books). Copy in I:FEc. The publication contains three instrumental compositions as follows:

[14] Canzon Francese detta la Carissima. a8
[15] [second chorus part-books] Canzon Francese del Secondo Tuono, detta la Galluppa. a4
[15] [first chorus part-books] Canzon Francese dell'Ottavo Tuono, detta la Sirifina. a4

Bargaglia, Scipion

Trattenimenti ossia divertimenti da suonare (Venezia, 1587). No extant copies are known.

Bariolla, Ottavio

CAPRICCI, OVERO CANZONI A'QUATTRO ... (Milano: Francesco & Simon Tini, 1594, in four part-books). Copy in I:Bc (incomplete, S and A only). This publication contains 20 canzonas for instrumental ensemble in four parts, the final three under the titles, *Famela Pietr' Antonio*, *Il Gobo Nan.*, and *La Todesca*.

Bellanda, Lodovico

CANZONETTE SPIRITUALI A DUE VOCI Con altre à Tre, & à Quattro da Sonare ... (Verona, Francesco dale Donne, et Scipione Vargnanosuo Genero, 1599, in two part-books). Copy in I:VEcap. This publication contains 9 vocal duos and 4 instrumental compositions in three and four parts as follows:

[12] (*Canzone*) Da Sonare a3 R.P. Ambrogio Bresciano

[14] (*Canzone*) Da Sonare a3 R.P. Ambrogio Bresciano
[16] (*Canzone*) Da Sonare a4
[18] (*Canzone*) Da Sonare a4

Buona, Valerio

IL SECONDO LIBRO DELLE CANZONETTE A TRE VOCI con l' aggionta di dodeci Tercetti a note ... (Venetia: Ricciardo Amadino, 1592, in three part-books). Copy in A:Wn. A modern edition is available from London Pro Musica. The original print contains 12 compositions for instrumental ensemble in three parts as follows:

[19] Ut
[20] Re
[21] Mi
[22] Fa
[23] Sol
[24] La
[25] La
[26] Sol
[27] Fa
[28] Hi
[29] Re
[30] Ut

Borgo, Cesare

Canzoni alla francese à 4. Lib. 2 ... (Venetia, 1599). This print of four part instrumental works has not survived.

Buus, Jacques

RECERCARI DI M. JACQUES BUUS Organista in Santo Marco di Venetia da cantare, & sonare d'Organo & altri Stromenti ... (Venetia: Antonio Gardane, 1547, in four part-books). Copies in BRD:Mbs and Rp. Contains 10 four-part 'recercars' for instruments.

IL SECONDO LIBRO DI RECERCARI DI M. JAQUES BUUS ORGANISTA In San Marco di Venetia da Cantare, & sonare d'Organo & altri Stromenti ... (Venetia:

Antonio Gardane, 1549, in four part-books). Copies
in BRD:Rp (incomplete: S, A, T only) and GB:Lbm
(incomplete: S, A, B only). Contains 8 four-part 'recerars'
for instruments.

Cavaccio, Giovanni

MUSICA DI GIOVANNI CAVACCIO DA BERGAMO, …
Canzoni alla Franzese, Pavana co'l Saltarello, Madrigali,
& un Proverbio non so se antico, o moderno. A QUAT-
TRO VOCI. (Venetia, 1597, in four part-books). Copy
in I:Bc. Contains four compositions with text in all
voices, and the following works for instrumental ensemble in four parts:

[1]   *La Bertani*
[2]   *La Nicolina*
[3]   *La Verità*
[4]   *La Lafranchina*
[5]   *La Brigientia*
[7]   *La Solcia*
[8]   *La Foresta*
[9]   *La Fina*
[11] *La Bignani*
[12] *La Nova*
[12] *La Morari*
[15] *La Villa chiara*
[16] *L'Agosta*
[17] *La Marina*
[18] *La Pasti*
[20] *La Benaglia*
[20] *La Massaina*
[22] *La Moiola*
[23] *L'Aresia*
[24] *Pavana*
[25] *Saltarello*
[26] *La Gastolda*

Conforti, Giovanni Battista

DI GIO. BATTISTA CONFORTI. *IL PRIMO LIBRO DE RICERCARI* a quattro Voci ... (Roma: Valerio Dorico, 1558, in four part-books). Copy in I:Bc; GB:Lbm and Lcm. Contains 1 three-part ricercar (folio 14v) and 14 four-part ricercars for instruments.

Gabrieli, Andrea

Sonate a cinque per istromenti (Venetia, Ang. Gardano, 1586). No copies survive.

MADRIGAL ET RICERCARI ... A Quattro voci ... (Venetia: Angelo Gardano, 1589, in four part-books). Contains 7 instrumental ricercars in four parts. Copy in CH:Bu. A second edition appeared in 1590, for which no complete copies are extant.

Gabrieli, Andrea and Giovanni

CONCERTI DI ANDREA, ET DI GIO: GABRIELI ORGANISTI DELLA SERENISS. SIG. DI VENETIA ... (Venetia, Angelo Gardano, 1587, in twelve part-books). Copies in A:Wn; BRD: F; I:Bc, Bsp, BRd, Sd, and TVcap. Contains 1 instrumental composition.

[I4v] *Ricercar per sonar* a8. Andrea Gabrieli

Gabrieli, Giovanni

Canzoni per sonare con ogni sorte di stromenti ... (Venice, 1608). Copy in BRD:As. A modern edition is available from Fort Hays Kansas State College (Music Series Nr. 2). Contains 4 canzonas (one called, *La Spiritata*) in four parts and 2 canzonas (*Fa sol la re* and *Sol sol la sol fa*) in eight parts by Gabrieli.

Gardane, Antonio (Publisher)

MOTETTA TRIUM VOCUM ... (Venetiis, Antonium Gardane, 1543, in three part-books). Copies in A:Wn and GB:Lbm. Contains 20 vocal compositions and 4 three-part instrumental works.

[D1v] *Re. Adrianus*
[D2] *Mi. Adrianus*
[D2v] *Fa. Adrianus*
[D3v] *Sol. Adrianus*

Ingegnieri, Marc'Antonio

IL SECONDO LIBRO DE' MADRIGALI ... CON DUE ARIE DI CANZON FRANcese per sonare ... (Venetia: Angelo Gardano, 1579, in four part-books). Copies in BRD:Mbs and I:Fn. A later edition appeared in 1584 for which a copy can be found in BRD:As. The original print contains 19 works with Italian text and 2 instrumental compositions.

[20] *Aria di Canzon* Francese per sonar del primo tono
[21] *Aria di Canzon* Francese per sonar del ottavo tono

Layolle, Francesco

Cinquanta canzoni (J. Moderne, 1540). Copy in BRD:W. According to Grove [10:568] this print contains four-part canzoni, although this composer's other works are for plucked strings.

Luzzaschi, Luzzascho

Ricercari di Luzzascho Luzzaschi à 4 (Venezia: Angelo Gardano, 158?). No copies are known to survive.

Malvezzi, Cristofano

DI CRISTOFANO MALVEZZI DA LUCCA ... *IL PRIMO LIBRO DE RECERCARI* à Quattro Voci ... (Perugia: Pietroiacomo Petrucci, 1577, in four part-books). Copy in I:Bc (incomplete: A, and an imperfect S and T). Contains 10 four-part ricercars for instruments.

Marino, Alessandro

DI ALESSANDRO MARINO, *IL PRIMO LIBRO DE MADRIGAL SPIRITUALI* ... Con una Canzone a dodeci nel fine ... (Venetia, Ricciardo Amadino, 1597, in part-books). Copy in I:Bc (incomplete: T only). Contains 1 instrumental composition.

[12v] *La bella Roncinetta*. Canzone a12

Maschera, Fiorenzo

LIBRO PRIMO DE CANZONI DA SONARE, A QUATTRO VOCI DI FLORENTIO MASCHERA ORGANISTA NEL DUOMO DI BRESCIA ... (Brescia: Vincenzo Sabbio, 1584, in four part-books). Copies in I:Bc and Bsp. Later editions can be found in GB:Lbm (1588), B:Br (1593), and I:Ac (1596). A modern edition is available from London Pro Musica.

- [1] *Canzon prima La Capriola*
- [2] *Canzon Seconda (La Martinenga)*
- [3] *Canzon Terza*
- [4] *Canzon Quarta*
- [5] *Canzon quinta La Maggia*
- [6] *Canzon Sesta*
- [7] *Canzon Settima (Al S. Pompeo Coradello)*
- [8] *Canzon Ottava*
- [9] *Canzon Nona (La Duranda)*
- [10] *Canzon Decima (La Rosa)*
- [11] *Canzon Undecima (L'Averolda)*
- [12] *Canzon Duodecima (L'Uggiera)*
- [13] *Canzon Decimaterza (La Girella)*
- [14] *Canzon Decimaquarta*

[15] *Canzon Decimaquinta*
[16] *Canzon Decimasesta*
[17] *Canzon Decimasettima*
[18] *Canzon Decimottava La Villachiara*
[19] *Canzon Decimanona*
[20] *Canzon Vigesima La Foresta*
[21] *Canzon Vigesimaprima*

Merulo, Claudio

IL PRIMO LIBRO DE RICERCARI DA CANTARE, A QUATTRO VOCI DI CLAUDIO MERULO DA CORREGGIO Organista in San Marco ... (Venetia: Antonio Gardano, 1574, in four part-books). Copies in F:Pn (incomplete: S, A, and B only) and I:Ac (incomplete: T only). The print contains 19 ricercars for instruments in four parts.

Padovano, Annibale

DI ANNIBALE PADOVANO, ORGANISTA Della Illustrissima S. di Venetia in San Marco, *Il Primo Libro de Ricercari* a quattro voci ... (Venetia: Antonio Gardano, 1556, in four part-books). Copy in GB:Lcm. There are no complete copies of a second edition (1588). The original print contains 13 ricercars in four parts for instruments.

Raval, Sebastiano

IL PRIMO LIBRO DI CANZONETTE A QUATTRO VOCI ... (Venetia: Giacomo Vincenti, 1593, in four part-books). Copy in I:Bc. Contains 3 ricercars for instruments in four parts.

Ruffo, Vicenzo

CAPRICCI IN MUSICA A TRE VOCI, DI VICENZO RUFFO MASTRO DI CAPELLA NEL DOMO DI MILANO ... (Melano [sic]: Francesco Moscheni, 1564, in three part-books). Copy in I:Rvat. A modern edition of six of these works is available from London Pro Musica.

[1] *La, Sol, Fa, Re, Mi*
[1v] *Quando'io penso al martire*
[2] *El Chiocho*
[3] *La Brava*
[3v] *La Gamba in Tenor*
[4] *Ut, Re, Me, Fa, Sol, La*
[4v] *Il Capriccioso*
[5] *O Felici occhi mei*
[6] *La disperata*
[6v] *Martin minoit son portiau au marche*
[8] *Dormendo un giorno*
[9v] *El Travagliato*
[10v] *La Gamba in Basso, & Soprano*
[11] *Hor ch'l cielo e la terra*
[11v] *La Danza*
[12v] *El Perfidioso*
[13] *Da bei rami scendea*
[13v] *El Pietoso*
[14] *El Malenaconico*
[14v] *Trinitas in unitate*
[15] *El Trapolato*
[15v] *El Cromato*
[16] *La Piva*

Scaletta, Orazio

AMOROSI PENSIERI IL SECONDO LIBRO De Madrigaletti A Cinque voci ... (Venetia: Girolamo Scotto, 1590, in four part-books). No complete copies are extant. The original print contained 1 four-part instrumental work.

[21] *La Quiricia Canzon Francese*

Sponga, Francesco

RICERCARI ET ARIE FRANCESI a Quattro Voci DI FRANCESCO SPONGA Discepolo di Andrea Gabrieli … (Venetia: Giacomo Vincenti, 1595, in four part-books). Copy in CH:Bu. Contains 14 ricercars and 4 works called 'Aria Francese,' for instrumental performance.

Stivori, Francesco

RICERCARI A QUATTRO VOCI, DI M. FRANCESCO STIVORI ORGANISTA DELLA MAGNIFICA Communità di Montagnana … (Venetia: Ricciardo Amadino, 1589, in four part-books). Copy in I:Bc (incomplete: S and A only). The print contained 21 ricercars for instrumental performance.

Il Secondo Libro de Ricercari a 4 voci … (Venezia: Amadino, 1594). This publication, formerly in USSR:K and now lost, contained 20 four-part instrumental ricercars.

RICERCARI CAPRICCI ET CANZONI A QUATTRO VOCI … (Venetia, Ricciardo Amadino, 1599, in four part-books). Copy in A:Wn (incomplete: S and A only). The publication contained 13 ricercars, 5 canzonas, and 3 capriccios for instrumental performance.

Tiburtino, Giuliano

FANTASIE, ET RECERCHARI A TRE VOCI, ACCOMODATE DA CANTARE ET SONARE PER OGNI INstrumento, Composte da M. Giuliano Tiburtino da Tievoli … (Venetiis: Hieronymum Scottum, 1549, in three part-books). Copy in GB:Lbm. The print contained the following three-part instrumental compositions.

[A1v] *Ut re mi fa sol la* (Tiburtino)
[A2] *La sol fa mi fa re la* (Tiburtino)
[A2v] *Fa re mi re sol mi fa mi* (Tiburtino)
[A2v] *Fa mi fa re ut* (Tiburtino)
[A3] *Sol sol sol ut* (Tiburtino)
[A3v] *Ut mi fa ut fa mi re ut* (Tiburtino)

[A3v]   *Re ut fa re fa sol la* (Tiburtino)
[A4]   *Re ut re fa mi re* (Tiburtino)
[A4v]   *Ut fa mi ut mi re ut* (Tiburtino)
[B1]   *Re fa mi re la* (Tiburtino)
[B1]   *Ut re mi ut fa mi re ut* (Tiburtino)
[B1v]   *La sol fa re mi* (Tiburtino)
[B2]   *Fantasia* (Tiburtino)
[C4v]   (*Ricercar*) Adriano Vuigliart [Willaert]
[D1v]   (*Ricercar*) Vuigliart
[D2v]   (*Ricercar*) Vuigliart
[D3v]   (*Ricercar*) Vuigliart
[D4v]   (*Ricercar*) Vuigliart
[E1v]   (*Ricercar*) Vuigliart
[E2v]   (*Ricercar*) Vuigliart
[E3v]   (*Ricercar*) Vuigliart

Viadana, Ludovico Grossi da

CANZONETTE A QUATRO VOCI … & un'aria di Canzon … (Venetia: Ricciardo Amadino, 1590, in four part-books). Copy in I:Bc (incomplete: S only). The publication contained 1 composition for instrumental ensemble.

[12v] *Aria di Canzon Francese* per sonar del primo tono. a4

Vecchi, Orazio

SELVA DI VARIA RICREATIONE DI HORATIO VECCHI … (Venetia: Angelo Gardano, 1590, in ten part-books). Copies in B:Br; BRD:Kl; and I:Bc, Bsp, and Fn. This publication consists almost entirely of music for lute and voices, but one composition seems to be intended for four-part instrumental ensemble.

[16v] *Fantasia*

Vicentino, Nicolò

MADRIGAL I A CINQUE VOCI ... (Milano: Paolo Gottardo Pontio, 1572, in five part-books). Copy in I:MOe. This publication contains Italian madrigals, together with one five-part composition for instrumental ensemble.

[22] *La bella.* Canzone da sonare

Vincenti, Giacomo (Publisher)

Musica spartita per Sonar (Venezia, Giacomo Vincenti, 158?). There are no known extant copies of this volume of instrumental music in score form.

Vinci, Pietro and Il Verso, Antonio

DI PIETRO VINCI SICILIANO Della Citta di Nicosia IL *SECONDO LIBRO DI MOTETTI, E RICERCARI* A TRE VOCI, Con alcuni Ricercari Di Antonio Il Verso suo Discepolo ... (Venetia: [Heirs of] Gierolamo Scotto, 1591, in three part-books). Copy in I:Vnm. This publication contains 7 ricercars by Vinci and 7 by il Verso.

SINGLE TITLE MANUSCRIPTS WITHOUT INSTRUMENT DESIGNATION

Dentice, Luigi (b. ca. 1510–1520, Naples)

[4] textless compositions in four parts. I:Fc (perhaps an autograph manuscript).

Gabrieli, Giovanni

[5] *Canzoni* I:Tn (MS. Foa III, L ii, 36, 40, 45, 49, and 51).

Canzon, a12. BRD:Kl.

Canzon a12 in echo. BRD:Kl.

Ricercar sopra Re fa mi don, a4. BRD:Kl.

Hodie Christus a mortuis, a12, for 3 vocal parts and 9 unspecified parts. BRD:Kl.

Gesualdo, Carlo (1561–1613)

Gagliarda, a4. I:Nc (MS. 4.6.3).

Guami, Giosoffo (c. 1540–1611, Lucca)

[2] *Canzoni*. GB:Lbm (MS. Add. 29427, ff. 9–12, 45–53).

[2] *Canzoni*, a4. I:VEcap (MS. 1128).

Porta, Constanzo (1528–1601, Padua)

Ricercar, a4. I:Bc (MS. U. 95).

SINGLE TITLE PRINTS DESIGNATED FOR WINDS

Buonavita, Antonia (late sixteenth century organist in Pisa)

Musik for 4 cornetti, 6 trombones, and organ, mentioned in 'Bartoli's announcement,' according to Eitner.[6]

[6] Robert Eitner, *Biographish-bibliographisches Quellen-Lexikon* (Leipzig: Breitkopf & Härtel, 1900).

Corteccia, Francesco

(Intermedii music for the inclusion in Antonio Landi's *Il Commodo*, performed for the wedding celebrations of Cosimo I, of Florence, and Eleanore of Toledo, in 1539). This music survives in an early print by Antonio Gardane (Venice, 1539): MUSICHE FATTE NELLE NOZZE DELLO ILLUSTRISSIMO DUCA DI FIRENZE IL SIGNOR COSIMO DE MEDICI … Copy in A:Wn, in five part-books. A modern edition is available by Andrew C. Minor and Bonner Mitchell, eds., *A Renaissance Entertainment* (Columbia: University of Missouri Press, 1968).

[iv] *Ingredere*. (for 4 voices, 4 cornetti, and 4 trombones)

[25] *Guardane almo pastore*, for cornett and 5 crumhorns; was repeated during the performance by these instruments together with singers.

[29] *Vientene almo riposo*, for alto voice and 4 trombones during the performance, but the Gardane publication cites it as for 'cinque voci cantata alla fine del quinto atto dalla notte, et sonata con quattro trombone.

Dalla Casa, Nicolò (d. Venice, 1617; brother to Girolamo Dalla Casa)

Canzoni et madrigali a quattro voci, libro secondo (Venice, 1591). Copy in A:Wn (incomplete).

SINGLE TITLE PRINTS WITHOUT INSTRUMENT DESIGNATION

Chiaula, Mauro (ca. 1544 – ca. 1603)

Sacrarum cantionum, quae octo tum vocibus, Tum ... instrumentis, chorisque coniunctis ac separatis, concini possunt, liber primus ... (1590). According to Grove,[7] this publication was for 8 voices, the title page indicating that instruments may double or replace the voices.

[7] Grove, 4:221.

Colombani, Orazio

Li dilettevo Magnificat ... accommodati per cantar, & sonar in concerto: con una a quatuordeci voci, a tre chori (Venezia: Giacomo Vencenti & Ricciardo Amadino, 1583). Copies in I:FEc and PCd.

Croce, Giovanni Dalla, Detto il Chiozzotto

Sonate a cinque (Venzia, 1580). No known copies are extant for this volume of instrumental ensemble music.

Gianotti, Giacomo (fl. 1584, Ravenna)

Canzoni ... raccolte per Francesco Rambaldi ... libro primo (Venice, 1584), contains 1 four-part canzona by Gianotti. Copy in BRD:Mbs (incomplete).

THE LOW COUNTRIES

Manuscript Collections Without Instrument Designation

I:Fc (MS. Basevi 2439, 'Basevi Codex'), ca. 1506–1514, Brussels, contains Isaac's instrumental ensemble composition, *La mi la sol*; Obrecht's *Missa Fortuna desperata*, with the incipit 'Fortuna' only; and one textless polyphonic work.

A:Wn (MS. 18746), signed Pierre Alamire, 1523, and sent to R. Fugger [the elder]. Five part-books contain more than 50 textless compositions for ensemble performance, some of vocal and some of instrumental origin.

A:Wn (MS. 18832), ca. 1523, as above. Two part-books containing 89 bicinia for instruments.

NL:SH (MS. 72.A), ca. 1530–1531, Flemish, contains 1 incomplete polyphonic textless composition.

F:CA (MS. 125–128), 1542, Bruges, copied for Zeghere van Male (1504–1601), a Bruges merchant. Four part-books contain 229 compositions, of which 11 are polyphonic textless works for instrumental ensemble.

NL:L (MS. 1441), ca. 1550–1567, Brussels, contains 1 polyphonic textless composition.

Print Collections Designated for Any Instrument

Baethen, J. (Publisher)

Dat ierste boeck van den nieuve duytsche Liedekens, met III. IIII. V. VI. ende VIII. partyen. Van excellente Musiciens nu corts in Musijcke ghestelt, bequaem om te singhen ende op instrumenten te spelen. (Maestricht: J. Baethen, 1554, in five part-books). Copy in BRD:HB. Contains 30 works by Clemens non papa (5), Episcopius (8), Evertz, Florius, Jordain, de Lattre, van der Müllen, Salmier, Wintelroy, Zaccheus and anonymous.

Phalèse, Pierre (Publisher)

Second livre des chansons a quatre parties ... convenables tant aux instrumentz comme a la voix. (Louvain: P. Phalèse, 1552, in four part-books). No complete copies are extant. The original print contained 30 compositions by Baston, Clemens non papa (6), Crecquillon (7), Crespel, Galli, Geerhart, Le Cocq, Le Jeune, Obrecht, Rogier, Waelrant, Wismes, and anonymous.

Tiers livre des chansons a quatre parties ... convenables tant aux instrumentz comme a la voix. (Louvain: P. Phalèse, 1552, in four part-books). No complete copies are extant. The original print contained 25 compositions by Baston (5), Caulery, Clemens non papa, Crecquillon, Crespel, De Lattre, Hailland , Janequin, Le Jeune, Lupi, Rore, Waelrant, and 3 anonymous. ·

Quatriesme livre des chansons a quatre parties ... convenables tant au instrumentz comme a la voix. (Louvain: P. Phalèse, 1552, in four part-books). No complete copies are extant. The original print contained 30 compositions by Baston, Caulery, Clemens non papa, Crecquillon (10), Crespel (5), Louys, de Manchicourt, Waelrant, and 4 anonymous.

Cincquiesme livre des chansons a quatre partie ... convenables tant aux instrumentz comme a la voix. (Louvain: P. Phalèse, 1552, in four part-books). No complete copies are extant. The original print contained 30 compositions by Baston, Buys, Cabilliau, Cardon, Clemens non papa, Crecquillon (15), Crespel, Galli, Gerard, Jacob, Wismes and 2 anonymous.

Premier livre des chansons a cincq et six parties ... convenables tant aux instrumentz comme à la voix. (Louvain: P. Phalèse, 1553, in five part-books). Copy in S:Uu. Contains 30 compositions by Baston, Canis, Chastelain, Clemens non papa (7), Crecquillon, Crespel, De Lattre, Galli,

Gheerkin, Hollander, Larchier, Rogier, Waelrant, and 2 anonymous. This work was reprinted in 1556; copies of this edition are in BRD:Kl and GB:Lbm.

Second livre des chansons a cincq et six parties ... convenables tant aux instrumentz comme à la voix. (Louvain: P. Phalèse, 1553, in five part-books). Copies in GB:Lbm and S:Uu. Contains 30 compositions by Bacchius, Baston, Briant, Canis, Clemens non papa (5), Crecquillon (7), Crespel, Hollandre, de Cocq, Louys, de Manchicourt, Martin Peu d'Argent, Cornel de Milan, Tubal, N. de Wismes, and 1 anonymous. This work was reprinted in 1560; a copy of this edition is in BRD:Kl.

Premier livre des chansons a quatre parties ... convenables tant aux instrumentz comme à la voix. (Louvain: P. Phalèse, 1554, in four part-books). Copy in BRD:Kl. Contains 31 compositions by Baston, Buys, Clemens non papa (5), Crecquillon H2), Crespel, Delatre, Gallus, Petit Jan, Loys, Morel, Pathie, Vaet, and Waelrant. This work was reprinted in 1558; a copy is in GB:Lbm.

Second livre des chansons a quatre parties ... convenables tant aux instrumentz comme à la voix. (Louvain: P. Phalèse, 1554, in four part-books). Copy in BRD:Kl. Contains 31 compositions by Baston, Clemens non papa (6), Crecquillon (7), Crespel, Gallus, Geraert, Le Cocq, Le Jeune, Obrecht, Pathie, Waelrant, Wismes, and 1 anonymous. This work was reprinted in 1559; a copy is in GB:Lbm.

Tiers livre des chansons a quatre parties ... convenables tant aux instrumentz comme à la voix. (Louvain, P. Phalèse, 1554, in four part-books). Copies in BRD:Kl and GB:Lbm. Contains 30 compositions by Baston, Caulery, Clemens non papa, Crecquillon (7), Crespel, Petit Jan, Heylanus, Janequin, Le Jeune , Lupi, da Rore, Waelrant, and 3 anonymous.

Cinquiesme livre des chansons a quatre parties ... convenables tant aux instrumentz comme à la voix. (Louvain: P. Phalèse, 1555, in four part-books). Copies in BRD:Kl and GB:Lbm. Contains 30 compositions by Baston,

Buys, Cabilliau, Cardon, Clemens non papa, Crecquillon (15), Crespel, Galli, Geraert, Jacob, de Wismes, and 2 anonymous.

Sixiesme livre des chansons à quatre parties, nouvellement composez et mises en musicque par maistre Jehan de Latre, maistre de chapelle ... Liége ... convenables tant aux instrumentz comme à la voix. (Lovain: par Pierre de la Phalyse, 1555). No copies are extant.

Septiesme livre des chansons a quatre, parties convenables tant aux instrumentz comme à la voix. (Louvain: P. Phalèse, 1560, in four part-books). Copy in GB:Och (incomplete: S and B only). Contains 35 anonymous compositions.

Septiesme livre de chansons a quatre parties convenables tant aux instruments comme à la voix. (Louvain: P. Phalèse, 1562, in four part-books). Copy in E:Mm. Contains 50 compositions by Barbion, Baston, Benedictus, Braquetz, Cadéac, Clemens non papa, Crecquillon (9), Godart, Gombert, Petit Jan, Pathie, Sandrin (6), Sermisy, Susato (3), and 15 anonymous.

Second livre des chansons a quatre et cinq parties ... convenables tant aux instrumens comme à la voix. (Louvain; P. Phalèse, 1570, in five part-books). Copies in BRD:Mbs, PL:GD, and S:Uu. Contains 27 compositions, by Lassus (20), de Monte and Rore.

Quatriesme livre des chansons a quatre cincq parties ... convenables tant aux instrumens comme à la voix. (Louvain: P. Phalèse, 1570, in five part-books). Copies in BRD:Mbs, PL:GD, and S:Uu. Contains 24 compositions by Lassus (23) and de Monte.

Septiesme livre des chansons a quatre parties ... Toutes convenables tant aux instruments qu'a la voix. (Louvain: P. Phalèse, 1570, in five part-books). Copies in DDR:ROu and S:Uu. Contains 50 compositions by Barbion, Baston, Benedictus, Berchem, Cadéac, Clemens non papa (8), Crecquillon (7), De Latre, Godard, Gombert, Pathie, Sandrin (8), and 17 anonymous.

Livre septiesme de chansons a quatre parties ... Toutes convenables tant aux instruments qu'a la voix. (Louvain: P. Phalèse, 1573, in four part-books). Copy in BRD:TRs. Contains 44 compositions by Barbion, Baston, Benedictus, Berchem, Cadéac, Clemens non papa (7) Crecquillon (6), De Lattre, Godard, Gombert, Pathie, Sandrin (4), and 18 anonymous.

Petit triésor des danses et branles à quatre et cinq Parties ... propres à jouer sur tous les estrumenz. (Louvain: chez Pierre Phalèse, libraire juré, 1573). No known copies are extant of this publication which contained four and five part compositions.

Madrigali a otto voci ... per cantar et sonar a due Chori ... (Antwerpen, P. Phalèse, 1596, in eight part-books). No complete copies exist for either this edition or its reprint in 1597. The original print contained 34 compositions.

Paradiso musicale di madrigali et canzoni a cinque voci ... (Antwerpen: P. Phalèse, 1596, in five part-books). Copies in F:Pn and GB:SH. Contains 40 compositions.

Phalèse, Pierre and Bellère, Jean (Publishers)

LIBER PRIMUS LEVIORUM CARMINUM ... Premier Livre de Danseries, contenant plusieurs Pavanes, PASSOMEZO, ALMANDES, GAILLIARDES, BRANLES, ETC. LE TOUT CONVENABLE SUR tous Instrumens Musicalz ... (Louvain: P. Phalèse; Antwerpen, J. Bellère, 1571, in four part-books). Copy in BRD:HB. Several modern editions include works from this print, including: H. Monkemeyer, *Lowener Tanzbuch* (Wilhelmshaven, 1962), E. Schmid, *Tanze des 16. Jahrhunderts fur vier Instrumenten* (1926), and E. Mohr, *Die Allemande* (Zurich, 1932). The original print contains compositions for instrumental ensemble in four parts as follows:

[2] *Fantasia*
[2] *Autre*
[2v] *Les Bouffons*
[2v] *De Post*
[2v] *Reprinse*

[2v]	*Dans de Hercules*
[3]	*Pavane Ferrareze*
[3v]	*Gailliarde Ferrareze*
[4]	*Pavane des Dieux*
[4]	*Gailliarde des dieux*
[4v]	*Pavane La garde*
[4v]	*La Gaillarde de La garde*
[5]	*Volte. Pour jouer a la fin de toutes gaillardes de ce ton*
[5v]	*Pavane j'ay du mal tant tant*
[5v]	*La gaillarde*
[6]	*Pavane Lesquercarde*
[6v]	*Pavane sur la bataille*
[6v]	*Gaillarde sur la bataille*
[7]	*Passomezo d'italye*
[7]	*Reprinse*
[7]	*La gaillarde (d'italye)*
[7v]	*Passomezo dangleterre*
[7v]	*La Reprinse*
[7v]	*Passomezo danvers*
[8]	*Passomeso la doulce*
[8]	*La Reprinse*
[8v]	*Passemezo du roy*
[8v]	*Reprinse*
[9]	*Almande prince*
[9]	*Almande smedelijn*
[9]	*Almande*
[9v]	*Almande*
[9v]	*La Reprinse*
[9v]	*Almande Savoye*
[10]	*Allmande de liege*
[10]	*Almande de liege*
[10]	*Allmande danvers*
[10v]	*Almande Lorayne*
[10v]	*Almande damours*
[10v]	*Almande*
[11]	*Almande*
[11]	*Almande*
[11v]	*Almande*
[11v]	*Almande*
[11v]	*Almande, courrante*
[12]	*Gaillarde Au joly boys*

[12]   *Gaillarde La Peronnelle*
[12v] *Gaillarde Mais pourquoy*
[12v] *Gaillarde Traditore*
[13]   *Gaillarde Si pour t'aymer*
[13v] *Gaillarde L'esmerillonne*
[13v] *Puisque vivre en servitude Gaillarde*
[14]   *Gaillarde La fanfare*
[14v] *Ce qui m'est deu & ordonné Gaillarde*
[14v] *Burate*
[15]   *La rocque Gaillarde*
[15]   *Gaillarde, francoise*
[15v] *Gaillarde. mon plaisir*
[15v] *L'Admiralle Gaillarde*
[16v] *Gaillarde d'escosse*
[16v] *Gaillarde*
[17]   *Gaillarde, La Brune*
[17]   *Gaillarde*
[17v] *Gaillarde la Vidasme*
[17v] *La basse gaillarde*
[18]   *Bransle de poytou simple*
[18]   *Bransle de poytou legier*
[18v] *Bransle du petit homme*
[18v] *Bransle legier double du petit homme*
[18v] *Le bransle du contraint*
[19]   *Bransle de la suitte du contraint legier*
[19]   *Bransle D'escosse*
[19]   *Bransle des Sabots*
[19v] *Quatre branles*
[19v] *Fagot*
[20]   *Den Hoboken dans*
[20]   *Ronde pourquoy*
[20v] *Bransle mon amy*
[20v] *Bransle*
[21]   *Bransle*
[21]   *Bransle*
[21v] *Premier Bransle Commune*
[21v] *2. Bransle*
[21v] *Premiere Bransle Gay*
[22]   *2. Bransle Gay*
[22]   *Premier Bransle de la guerre*
[22]   *2. Bransle*

[22v] *Premier bransle de Champaigne*
[22v] *2. Bransle*
[22v] *3. Bransle*
[23] *4. Bransle*
[23] *5. Bransle*
[23v] *6. Bransle*
[23v] *7. Bransle*
[23v] *8. Bransle*
[24] *Premier Bransle de Bourgoigne*
[24] *2. Bransle*
[24v] *3. Bransle*
[24v] *4. Bransle*
[24v] *5. Bransle*
[25] *6. Bransle*
[25] *7. Bransle*
[25v] *8. Bransle*
[25v] *9. Bransle*
[25v] *10. Bransle*
[26] *11. Bransle*
[26] *12. Bransle*
[26v] *13. Bransle*
[26v] *14. Bransle*
[26v] *15. Bransle*
[27] *16. Bransle*
[27v] *17. Bransle*
[27v] *18. Bransle*
[28] *Bransle des Lavandieres*
[28] *Bransle Hauberrois*
[28] *Bransle Guillemette*

Livre de musicque, contenant plusieurs excellentes chansons et motettz a deux parties, convenables a tous instrumens musicalz … (Louvain: P. Phalèse; Antwerpen: J. Bellère, 1571, in two part-books). Copies in BRD:Mbs and DDR:ROu. A modern edition of this print is available from Edition Hoeck (Heft 5) The original print contains 73 compositions by Turnhout (13), Verdonck (9), and 51 anonymous.

Een duytsch Musyck Boeck, daer inne begrepen syn vele schoone Liedekens met IIII. Met V. ende VI. Partijen … Ghecomponeert bij diversche excellente Meesters seer lusticb om singben ende spelen op alle in instrumenten (Louvain: P. Pbalèse; Antwerpen, J. Bellère, 1572, in five part-books). Copy in BRD:Mbs. Contains 33 compositions by Jan Belle (6), Clemens non papa (5), de Latre, Episcopius (7), Evertz, Faignient, Hellinck, Van der Muelen, Stockaert, G. Turnhout, J. Turnhout, Wintelroy, and anonymous.

Livre septieme des chanssons a quatre parties ... accommodées tant aux instruments, comme à la voix ... (Louvain: P. Phalèse; Anvers J. Bellère, 1576, in four part-books). No complete copies of this print are extant, but it is thought that this is identical with a print by the same title of 1589 (Copy in S:Skma (incomplete: S, T, and B only), which was reprinted in 1592 (Copy in F:Pthibault), 1597 (Copies in BRD:Kl and Rp), 1601 and 1605 (no complete copies), and 1609 (Copies in GB:Lbm and LI). The 1589 print contains 44 compositions by Arcadelt, Baston, Benedictus, Berchem, Cadéac, Clemens non papa, Costeley, Crecquillon (7), Donato, Godart, Gombert, de Latre, Pathie, Sandrin (8), Sermisy, Waelrant (4), and 8 anonymous.

CHOREARUM MOLLIOROM COLLECTANEA ... RECUEIL DE DANSERIES, CONTENANT PRESQUE TOUTES SORTES DE DANSES, comme Pavanes, Pass'emezes, Allemandes, Gaillardes, Branles, & plusieurs autres, accommodées aussi bien a la Voix, comme à tous Instrumens Musicaux, nouvellement amass' d' aucuns sçavans maistres Musiciens, & autres amateurs de toute sorte d'Harmonie. (Anvers: P. Phalèse ... & Jean Bellère ... 1583, in four part-books). Copies in BRD:KNu and Mbs. A modern edition of some of these dances was prepared by H. Mönkemeyer (*Antwerpene Tanzbuch*, Wilhelmshaven, 1962). In the original print all the titles were for instrumental ensemble in four parts as follows:

[2]   *Caro Ortolano*
[2]   *Saltarello*
[2v] *Pass'e mezzo d'Italie*
[3v] *Represa*

[3v]   *Saltarello*
[4]   *Represa*
[4v]   *Pass'e mezzo Moderno*
[5v]   *Represa*
[6]   *Salterello*
[6]   *Represa*
[6v]   *Passomezo d'Angleterre*
[6v]   *La Reprinse*
[6v]   *Passomezo d'Anvers*
[7]   *Passomeso la doulce*
[7]   *La Reprinse*
[7v]   *Pass'e mezzo della Paganina*
[7v]   *Salterello*
[8]   *Pavane Ferrareze*
[8v]   *Gaillarde Ferrareze*
[9]   *Pavane J'ay du mal*
[9]   *La Gaillarde*
[9v]   *Pavane de la Bataille*
[10]   *Gaillarde de la Battaille*
[10v] *Gaillarde Au joly bois*
[10v] *Gaillarde (du ton de la guerre)*
[11]   *Gaillarde Ce qui m'est deu*
[11]   *Gaillarde La Peronelle*
[11v] *Gaillarde Mais pourquoy*
[11v] *Gaillarde Traditore*
[12]   *Gaillarde Si pour t'aymer*
[12v] *Gaillarde L'esmerillonne*
[12v] *Gaillarde Puisque vivre*
[13]   *Gaillarde La fanfare*
[13v] *Gaillarde La roque el fuso*
[14]   *Gaillarde Francoise*
[14]   *Gaillarde Mon plaisir*
[14v] *Gaillarde l'Admiralle*
[15]   *Gaillarde d'Escosse*
[15]   *Gaillarde*
[15v] *Gaillarde Brunette*
[15v] *Ballo Milanese*
[16]   *Gaillarde la Lavandara*
[16v] *Almande Poussinghe*
[16v] *Saltarello*
[17]   *Almande*

[17]   *La Reprinse*
[17v] *Almande*
[17v] *Saltarello*
[18]   *Almande d'Amour*
[18v] *Almande Bruynsmedelijn*
[18v] *Saltarello*
[19]   *Almande de Liege*
[19v] *Almande*
[19v] *Saltarello*
[20]   *Almande*
[20]   *Almande*
[20v] *Almande Loreyne*
[20v] *Saltarello*
[21]   *Almande Bisarde*
[21v] *Almande Fortune helas pourquoy*
[22]   *Almande de Don Frederico*
[22v] *Almande Spiers*
[23]   *L'arboscello ballo Furlano*
[23v] *Ballo Anglese*
[23v] *Saltarello*
[24]   *Ungaresca*
[24]   *Saltarello*
[24v] *La Parma*
[24v] *Saltarello*
[25]   *Putta Nera Ballo Furlano*
[25]   *Schiarazula Marazula*
[25v] *Branle simple*
[25v] *Branle 2*
[25v] *Branle 3*
[25v] *Branle 4*
[26]   *Branle 5*
[26]   *Branle 6*
[26v] *Premier Branle de Gay*
[26v] *Branle 2*
[26v] *Branle 3*
[27]   *Branle 4*
[27]   *Branle 5*
[27]   *Branle 6*
[27v] *Branle (commun)*
[27v] *Branle 2*
[27v] *Branle 3*

[28]   *Branle 4*
[28]   *Branle 5*
[28v] *Branle 6*
[28v] *Branle 7*
[28v] *Branle 8*
[29]   *Branle 9*
[29]   *Branle 10*
[29v] *Branle de Poictou*
[29v] *Branle 2*
[29v] *Branle 3*
[30]   *Branle 4*
[30]   *Branle 5*
[30]   *Branle 6*
[30v] *Branle 7*
[30v] *Branle 8*
[31]   *Branle de Champaigne*
[31]   *Branle 2*
[31]   *Branle 3*
[31v] *Branle 4*
[31v] *Branle 5*
[31v] *Branle 6*
[32]   *Branle 7*
[32]   *Branle 8*
[32]   *Branle 9*
[32v] *Branle pourquoy*
[32v] *Branle mon amy*
[33]   *Branle 2*
[33]   *Premier Branle de la guerre*
[33]   *Branle 2*
[33v] *Quatre branles*
[33v] *Les Fagots*
[34]   *Hoboken dans*
[34]   *Autre*
[34v] *Branle de petit homme*
[34v] *Branle legier*
[34v] *Branle du contraint*
[35]   *Branle de la suite du contraint*
[35]   *Branle d'Escosse*
[35]   *Branle des Sabots*
[35v] *Branle de Poitou simple*
[35v] *Branle de poitou legier*

La fleur des chansons d'Orlande de Lassus ... a quatre, cinc, six & huit parties, accomodées tant aux instrumens comme a la voix ... (Antwerpen: P. Phalèse & J. Bellère, 1592, in five part-books). No complete copies are extant of this edition, but copies of a reprint (1596) are in PL:GD and BRD:W. The original print contained 77 works by Lassus and 1 by Rore.

Chansons a cinc parties de M. Iean Pierre Svvelingh...et Cornille Verdonq ... accomodées tant aux instruments, comme à la voix ... (Antwerpen: P. Phalèse et J. Bellère, 1594, in five part-books). Copies in GB:Ob (incomplete: S, T, B, and 5 only) and NL:Avnm (incomplete: A only). This print contains 18 compositions by Sweelinck and 4 by Verdonck.

Susato, Tielman (Publisher)

Vingt et six chansons musicales ... a cincq parties, convenables tant a la voix comme aussi prop ices a jouer de divers instruments ... (Antwerpen: T. Susato [1543], in four part-books). Copies in A:Wn, B:Br, BRD:B and BE, GB:Lbm, and S:Uu. Contains 26 compositions by Baston, Canis, Crecquillon (5), Descaudain, Gallus, Gombert, Lupi, Mouton, Richafort, Susato (5) and anonymous.

Premier livre des chansons a quatre parties ... convenables tant la voix comme aux instrumentz ... (Antwerpen, T. Susato, 1543, in four part-books). Copies in A:Wn, B:Br, BRD:B and Mbs, GB:Lbm, and S:Uu. Contains 31 compositions by Baston, Canis, Clemens non papa, Crecquillon (6), Gombert, J. de Hollande, Lupi, Pathie, Pieton, Roucourt, Susato (8), and anonymous.

Le second livre des chansons a quatre parties ... convenables tant a la voix comme aux instrumentz ... (Antwerpen: T. Susato, 1544, in four part-books). Copies in A:Wn, BRD:B and Mbs, GB:Lbm, and S:Uu. Contains 31 compositions by Canis, Crecquillon, Gallus, Gombert, Le Cocq (6), Lupi, de Manchicourt (5), Payen, Sandrin, Susato (3), and anonymous.

Le tiers livre de chansons a quatre parties (composees par Maistre Thomas Cricquillon maistre de la Chapelle de l'empereur) … convenables tant a la voix comme aulx instrumentz … (Antwerpen: T. Susato, [1544], in four part-books). Copies in A:Wn, B:Br, BRD:B and Mbs, GB:Lbm, and S:Uu. Contains 36 works by Crecquillon and 1 by Le Cocq.

Le quatriesme livre des chansons a quatre parties … convenables tant a la voix comme aux instrumentz … (Antwerpen: T. Susato, 1544, in four part-books). Copies in A:Wn, BRD:B and Mbs, S:Uu. Contains 34 compositions by Barbé, Baston, Benedictus, Canis, Certon, Courtois, Crecquillon, Gallus, Gerardus, Goddart, Gombert (6), Le Cocq, Lescornet, de Manchicourt, Sermisy, Susato (4), van Wilder, Willaert, and anonymous.

Le cincquiesme livre (des chansons) … convenables et propices a jouer de tous instrumentz … (Antwerpen: T. Susato, 1544, in five part-books). Copies in A:Wn, BRD:B and Mbs, and GB:Lbm. Contains 32 compositions by Baston, Benedictus, Canis (6), Gallus, Gombert (11), Josquin, Larchier, Lupi, Richafort, Willaert, and anonymous.

Le sixiesme livre contenant trente et une chansons nouvelles a cincq et a six parties convenables et prop ices a jouer de tous instrumentz … (Antwerpen: T. Susato, 1545, in five part-books). Copies in A:Wn, B:Br, BRD:B, BE, and Mbs, and GB:Lbm. Contains works by Balduin, Benedictus, Courtois, Crecquillon (6), Gombert, Larchier, Le Cocq, de Manchicourt, Mouton, Susato (3), P. v. Wilder, Willaert, and 2 anonymous.

Le huitiesme livre des chansons a quatre parties … convenables tant a la voix comme aux instrumentz … (Antwerpen, T. Susato, 1545, in four part-books). Copies in A:Wn, BRD:B and Mbs, GB:Lbm, and S:Uu. Contains 37 compositions by Baston, Canis, Clemens non papa (9), Crecquillon (8), Havericq, Richafort, de Rore, and 5 anonymous.

L'unziesme livre contenant vingt et neuf chansons amoureuses a quatre parties, propices a tous instrumentz musicaulx ... (Antwerpen: T. Susato, 1549, in four part-books). Copies in A:Wn, BRD:B and Mbs, DDR:Bds, and GB:Lbm. Contains 31 works by Baston, Clemens non papa (8), Crecquillon (7), Crespel, Guyot, de Hollandre, Josquin, Morel, Recourt, Susato (5), and anonymous.

Le douzieisme livre contenant trente chansons amoureuses a cincq parties. Propices a tous instrumentz musicaulx ... (Antwerpen: T. Susato, 1550, in five part-books). Copies in BRD:Mbs and GB:Lbm. This work was reprinted in 1558; a copy can be found in A:Wn. The original print contained 30 compositions by Barbiou, Baston, Canis, Crecquillon, Clemens non papa (8), Gallus, Gerard, Gombert (7), Hanache, de Hollande, Le Roy, and 2 anonymous.

Le treziesme livre contenant vingt et deux chanson nouvelles a six et a huyt parties. Propices a tous instrumentz musicaulx ... (Antwerpen: T. Susato, 1550, in five part-books). Copy in BRD:Mbs. Contains 22 compositions by Castileti (6), Clemens non papa, Gallus, Gombert, Hollander, Larchier, Manchicourt, Rore, Willaert, and 3 anonymous.

Het ierste musyck boexken mit vier partyen ... zeer lustich am singen en spelen op alle musicale Instrumenten ... (Antwerpen: T. Susato, 1551, in four part-books). No complete copies are extant. Contained 28 compositions by Barbé, Baston, Geerhart, Hellinck, Susato (4), Vinders, Souliaert, and 15 anonymous.

Het tvueetste musick boexken mit vier partyen ... zeer lustich om singen en spelen op alle musicale Instrumenten ... (Antwerpen: T. Susato, 1551, in four part-books). No complete copies are extant. Contained 27 works by Appenzeller, Baston (5), Clemens non papa, Ghiselin, Hellinck, Souliaert (5), Susato (2), and 11 anonymous.

Het derde musyck boexken ... danserye, te vuetens Basse dansen, Ronden, Allemaingien, Pavanen ende meer andere, mits oeck vyfthien nieuwe gaillarden, zeer lustich ende bequaem am spelen op alle musicale Instrumenten ... (Antwerp: T. Susato ['at the sign of the Crumhorn'], 1551, in four part-books). Copies in E:Mmc (incomplete: T only) and NL:DHgm (incomplete: S only). Modern editions are available by F.J. Giesbert (Schott's Sohne (Heft I: Edition Schott 2435 and Heft II: Edition Schott 2436) and European American Music (1936). This publication of instrumental ensemble music is almost certainly drawn in part from the repertoire of the Antwerp Civic Wind Band, of which Susato was the leader.

[2]   *Bergerette Dont vient cela*
[2]   *Reprise*
[2v] *Bergeret (sans roch)*
[3]   *Reprise*
[3]   *Reprise aliud*
[3v] *Reprise Cest une dure despartie*
[4]   *Bergerette*
[4]   *La morisque*
[4v] *Les grands douleurs. Bergerette*
[5]   *Entre du fol*
[5v] *Danse du Roy*
[5v] *Le joly boys*
[6]   *Mon desir. Basse danse*
[6v] *Reprise Le cueur est bon*
[7]   *Reprise*
[7v] *Den iersten ronde. Pourquoy*
[7v] *Den II . ronde . Mon amy*
[8]   *Den III. ronde*
[8]   *Den IIII. ronde*
[8v] *Den V. ronde. Wo bistu*
[8v] *Den VI. ronde*
[9]   *Den VII. ronde. Il estoit une fillette*
[9]   *Den VIII. ronde . Mille ducas en vostre bource*
[9v] *Den IX. ronde*
[9v] *Aliud*
[9v] *Saltarelle*
[10] *Les quatre branles*
[10] *Fagot*
[10] *Den hobaecken dans*
[10v] *De post*

[10v] *Reprise*
[10v] *De matrigale*
[10v] *Danse de Hercules oft maticine*
[11] *Den iersten Allemaingne*
[11] *Recoupe*
[11] *Den tweeden Allemaingne*
[11v] *Den III. Allemaingne*
[11v] *Den IIII. Allemaingne*
[12] *Den V. Allemaingne*
[12] *Den VI. Allemaingne*
[12v] *Den VII. Allemaingne*
[12v] *Den VIII. Allemaingne*
[12v] *Recoupe*
[12v] *Recoupe aliud*
[13] *Pavane. Mille regretz*
[13] *Pavane. La dona*
[13] *Pavane. Mille ducas*
[13v] *Pavane. Si par souffrir*

La Fleur de chansons et quatriesme livre à quatre La parties, ... propices a tous instrumentz musicaulx ... (Antwerpen: T. Susato, [1552], in four part-books). No complete copies survive. The original print contained 27 works by Appenzeller, Canis, Clemens non papa, Crecquillon, Crespel, Gombert, Guyot, de Hollande, de Lattre, Le Roy, Millet, Pathie, Wilder, Willaert, and 6 anonymous.

Fleur de chansons et cinquiesme livre à trios parties, ... propices a tous instrumentz musicaulx ... (Antwerpen: T. Susato, 1552, in three part-books). Copy in A:Wn. The print contains 26 compositions by Baston, Crecquillon (16), Gombert, Janequin (7), and anonymous.

La Fleur de chansons et sixiesme livre à troix parties, ... propices a tous instrumentz musicaulx ... (Antwerpen: T. Susato [1552], in three part-books). No complete copies are extant. The original print contained 23 works by Appenzeller, Cabillau, Canis, Crespel (6), Gombert, Janequin, Jonckers, and 7 anonymous.

Waelrant, H. and Laet, J. (Publishers)

Jardin musiqual, contenant plusieurs belles fleurs de chansons, choysies d' entre les oeuvres ... propices tant a la voix comme aux instruments. Le premier livre. (Antwerpen: H. Waelrant & J. Laet, [1556], in four part-books). Copies in BRD:As and Mbs. Contains 24 compositions by Barbion, Baston, Bracquet, Caulery, Chastelain, Crecquillon (5), Clemens non papa, Crespel, Dambert, Petit Jan de Latre, O. de Latre, Hauricq, Janequin, Le Roy, Tubal, and Vaet.

Jardin musical ... tant propices a la voix comme aux instrumetz. Livre second. (Antwerpen: H. Waelrant & J. Laet, [1556], in four part-books). Copies in BRD:As and Mbs. Contains 26 works by Bacchius, Bracquet, Caulery (11), Clemens non papa, Crecquillon, Galli, Maillard, Tubal, Waelrant, and anonymous.

Jardin musical, ... propices tant a la voix, comme aux instruments. Le tiers livre. (Antwerpen: H. Waelrant & J. Laet, [1556], in four part-books). Copies in BRD:As and Mbs. Contains 27 compositions by Cabiliau, Caulery, Chastelain, Clemens non papa, Crecquillon, Crespel, Janequin, Molet, Moreau, Tubal, Waelrant, and 5 anonymous.

SINGLE TITLE MANUSCRIPTS WITHOUT INSTRUMENT DESIGNATION

Clemens, Johann 'non papa'

Forbons, five voices. NL:Uu (K.xii.104)

Hortens, four voices. NL:Uu (K.xi.101)

Justempus, four voices. NL:Uu (K.xi.103)

Lutens, four voices. NL:Uu (K.xi.102)

Resueilles vous, five voices. NL:Uu (K.xi.120)

[3] [untitled], four voices. NL:Uu (P-C.Mus. 242, K.xi, 107, 109, 111)

Single Title Prints Without Instrument Designation

Castro, Jean de

Chansons et madrigales à quatre parties, convenables tant à la voix comme à touttes sortes d'instrumens. (Leuven: Pierre Phalèse, 1570, in four part-books). Copies in DDR:ROu and S:Uu.

Chansons, odes, et sonetz de Pierre Ronsard ... (Leuven: P. Phalèse; Antwerpen: J. Bellère, 1576, in five part-books). Copies in BRD:Mbs and Kl, and S:Uu.

Livre de chansons à cinq parties, convenable tant à la voix, comme à toutes sortes d'instrumens: avec une pastorelle à VII. en forme de dialogue. (Antwerpen P. Phalèse, 1586, in five part-books). Copy in BRD:Mbs.

Cornet, Séverin

Canzoni (Antwerp, Joannem Latii, 1563). No copies are known to survive.

Peetrino, Jacobo

DI JACOBO PEETRINO DE MALINES *IL PRIMO LIBRO DE MADRIGALI* A QUATRO VOCI ... (Venetia: Angelo Gardano, 1583, in four part-books). Copy in I:Vnm (incomplete: S, T, B only). Contains 1 work for instrumental ensemble in four parts.

[21] *Aria Francese* per sonare

POLAND

Manuscript Collections Without Instrument Designation

PL:Kk (MS. D. 25–27), late sixteenth century, Kraków, in three part-books. Contains 1 polyphonic textless composition.

SPAIN

Manuscript Collections Without Instrument Designation

E:SE (without shelfmark), ca. 1500, contains more than 200 compositions in two to five parts, mostly with only a text incipit for identification; some of instrumental origin.

E:Boc (MS. 5 [12-VI-12]), early sixteenth century, contains 4 polyphonic textless compositions.

E:Sc (MS. 5-5-20), early sixteenth century, probably Seville, contains 1 polyphonic textless composition.

E:V (MS. 17), mid-sixteenth century, contains 7 polyphonic textless compositions.

E:Mmc (MS. 13230), second-half, sixteenth century, contains 1 polyphonic textless composition.

US:BLl (MS. 1), 1582, Guatemala, contains 2 polyphonic textless compositions.

US:BLl (MS. 2), 1582, Guatemala, contains 3 polyphonic textless compositions.

E:Bc (MS. 588/1), ca. 1595, in three part-books, contains 1 polyphonic textless composition.

E:GRcr (MS without shelfmark [Lóp. AM Nr. 5]), ca. 1598, Granada, contains 4 instrumental works in five parts, probably by Aambrosio Cotes (ca. 1550–1603, Seville). A modern edition of these works was made by J. Climent, ed., *Tesoro sacro musical* (1971).

US:BLl (MS. 6), late sixteenth century, Guatemala, contains 3 polyphonic textless compositions.

US:BLl (MS. 8), late sixteenth century, Guatemala, contains 26 polyphonic textless works.

US:BLl (MS. 9), late sixteenth century, Guatemala, contains 2 polyphonic textless compositions.

E:Bim (MS. M. 34), ca. 1601, Toledo, contains 1 polyphonic textless composition.

SWITZERLAND

Manuscript Collections Without Instrument Designation

CH:SGa (MS. 462), early sixteenth century, contains 5 polyphonic textless compositions.

CH:Bu (MS. AN. II. 46), early sixteenth century, from a monastery in Kleinbasel, contains 1 polyphonic textless composition.

BRD:Mu (MS. 20/ Art. 239), ca. 1514–1517, Basel, contains 1 French secular work without text.

CH:Bu (MS. F. X. 1–4), 1522–1524, contains several French secular compositions with text incipits only.

BRD:Mu (MS. 80/322–325), 1527, Basel, contains 2 polyphonic textless compositions.

CH:Bu (MS. F.X. 21), ca. 1529–1575, contains several German and Italian works with incipits only.

CH:Bu (MS. F. X. 5–9), ca. 1535–1546, in five part-books, contains 4 polyphonic textless compositions and several French secular works with incipits only.

CH:SGa (MS. 463, 'Tschudi Liederbuchn'), ca. 1540, Glarus, two of the original four part-books, contains 4 polyphonic textless compositions and 1 dance, *Pavanna*.

CH:Bu (MS. F. IX. 32–35), ca. 1546–1547, four part-books, contains 1 polyphonic textless composition.

CH:Bu (MS. F. IX. 59–62), after 1550, four part-books, contains many German secular works with text incipits only.

CH:Bu (MS. F. X. 17–20), after 1550, four part-books, contains several Italian compositions with incipits only.

Index

Index of Names

A

Abell, Dav., 16th century composer, 25
Adorno, Francesco, 16th century Florentine composer, 38
Agostini, Lodovico, 1534–1590, Italian composer, 88
Agricola, Martin, 1486–1556, German composer, 17, 76
Aich, Arnt von, publisher, in Köln ensemble collection of 1519, 61
Aichinger, Gregor, 1564–1628, German composer, 65, 78
Al Sfoi, composer in 1585 4-part canzone, 82
Alamire, Pierre, 1470–1536, German/Dutch composer of works for Fugger, 106
Albert, Duke of Prussia, 16th century wind band collection, 57
Albrecht v, Duke of Bararia, 10
Alessandrino, Venetiano, 16th century composer, 29
Amadino, Ricciardo, 16th century publisher in Venice, 82, 89, 94, 98, 101ff, 105
Amsfortius, Franciscus, 16th century composer, 25
Anselmo, 16th century composer, 30
Antonie Brumel, 1460–1613, French composer, 11
Apel, Jakob, 16th century publisher in Leipzig, 65
Appenzeller, Benedictus, 1480–1558, Franco-Flemish composer, 120, 122
Arbau, Thoinot, 1520–1595, French author of *Orchésographie*, 56
Arcadelt, Jacques, 1507–1568, Flemish composer, 25, 30, 49, 63, 114
Arrivabene, Andrea, 1540 publisher of 4-part ensemble music, 92
Arthopius, Balthasar, ca. 1490–1534, German composer, 63
Ashton, Hugh, d. 1522, composer of Hornpype, 35ff
Ashwell, 16th century composer, 35
Attaingnant, Pierre, ca. 1494–1552, Parisian publisher, 38ff, 40, 42ff, 44ff, 47, 50ff

B

Bacchius, 16th century composer, 108, 123
Baethen, J., publisher of 1554 book of instrumental partitas, 106
Balduin, Noel, 1480–1530, German composer, 63, 119
Banchieri, Adriano, 1568–1634, Italian composer, 85, 93
Barbé, 16th century composer, 63, 119ff
Barbion, 16th century composer, 109ff, 120, 123
Bargaglia, Scipion, composer in 1587, 93
Barges, composer in 1551 collection of 3-part canzoni, 92
Bariolla, Ottavio, 16th century composer, 93
Barley, Willim, 16th century publisher in London, 33
Barre, Antonio, 16th century composer, 30
Bassano, Giovanni, 16th century composer, 88ff
Baston, Josquin, 1515–1576, Franco-Flemish composer, 25, 107ff, 109, 114, 118ff, 123
Battagh, Mario of Rimini, 15th century, 8
Bauer, Conrad, 17th century publisher in Nürnberg, 66
Bauldouyn, 16th century composer, 64
Baumann, Georg, 16th century publisher in Erfurt, 65, 72ff
Beaujoyeulx, Ballthasar de, French composer for Henry III of France, 55
Becker, Carl, 16th century composer in German dance music ['Duke Moritz'], 76
Belin, Guillaume, 16th century composer, 44ff, 48ff
Bellanda, Lodovico, fl. 1593–1613, Italian composer, 93
Belle, Jan, 16th century Italian composer, 114
Bellère, Jean, 16th century publisher in Antwerpen, 110, 114ff, 124
Bendusi, Francesco, d. 1553, Italian composer, 89
Benedictus, (Appenzeller?) 16th century composer, ca. 1544–1576, 39,63, 109ff 113, 119
Benoist, Nicolo, b. ca. 1510, composer, 63, 92
Berchem, Jacob van, 1505–1567, Franco-Flemish composer, 25,49, 92, 109ff, 114
Berg & Neuber, 16th century publishers in Nürnberg, 64
Berg, Adam, 16th century publisher in Munich, 65, 67, 69, 73ff
Berg, Johann, 16th century publisher in Erben, 62, 66
Bergen, Gimel, 16th century Dresden publisher, 72, 74
Bergs, Johann, widow of Dietrich Gerlach, 16th century German publisher, 73ff
Biffi, Gioseffo, 1596, German publisher, 79
Binchois, Giles, 1400–1460 Franco-Flemish composer, 8
Bischoff, 16th century composer, 65
Blanckmüller, Georg, 16th century composer, 62ff, 76
Blancks, Edward, 16th century composer, 36
Bohemus (Martin de Boémia?), 16th century composer, 62
Bologna, Jeronimo da, 16th century composer, 92
Borgo, Casare, 16th century Milanese organist, composer, 94
Botsch, 16th century German composer, 62
Bourguignon, Anónim, ca. 1450–1521, Franco-Flemish composer, 38, 43, 49
Boyvin, Jacques, 1562–1633, French composer, 44, 48ff
Brack, 16th century German composer, 61ff
Bracquet, 16th century composer, 123
Braetel, Huldrich, 1495–1544 German composer, 25

Bramieri, 16th century composer, 61
Brandt, Lüdeken, 16th century publisher in Helmstedt, 67
Brant von, Jobst, 1517–1570, German composer, 63ff
Braquetz, 16th century composer, 109
Brätel, 16th century German composer, 63
Breitengraser, Wilhelm, 16th century German composer, 62ff
Bresciano, Ambrogio, late 16th century Italian composer, 93ff
Briant, Denis, 16th century composer, 25, 108
Bridam, 16th century composer, 39
Brimle, John, ca. 1500–1576, English composer, 35
Brixia, Matheus de, fl. 1412–1419 in Vicenza, composer, 13
Bruck, Arnold von, 1500–1554, Franco-Flemish composer, 62ff
Bruyer, 16th century composer, 63
Bultel, Jacob, 16th century composer, 25
Buona (Bona?), Valerio, b. 1560, composer, 94
Buonavita, Antonia, late 16th ca. organist in Pisa, composer, 104
Burck, Joachim, composer in 1575, 65
Busnois, Antoine, 1430–1492, French composer, 31
Buus, Jacques, 1500–1565, Franco-Flemish composer, 82, 94
Buys, 16th century composer, 107ff

C

Cabillau, 16th century composer, 107, 109, 122ff
Cadéac, Pierre, fl. 1530–1558, French composer, 45, 109ff, 114
Caietain (Cajetan), Fabrice Martin (fl. 1570–1578), 56
Calabr, Andreas Tallafangi, fl. 1440–1450, composer, 13
Calenius, Gerwinus, 16th century publisher in Köln, 67
Canis, Cornelius, 1510–1561, Franco-Flemish composer, 25, 107ff, 118ff, 122
Cardon, 16th century composer, 107, 109
Castellani, Margherita of Florence, ca. 1465, 14
Castileti, Johannes, 1512–1588, Flemish composer, 25, 120
Castro, Jean de, 1540–1611, Belgian composer, 124
Caulery, Jean, 16th century composer, 107ff, 123
Causton, Thomas, early 16th century English composer, 35
Cavaccio, Giovanni, 1556–1626, Italian composer, 95
Cavazzoni, Hieronimo, 16th century composer, 92
Certon, Pierre, 1510–1572 French composer, 38, 43ff, 49ff, 119
Chabril, 16th century composer, 82
Champernowne, Sir Richard, maintained wind band with Holborne, 33
Chastelain, Joannes, 16th century composer, 25, 107, 123
Chaussee, Nivelle de la, owned a Chansonnier, 15th century, 8
Chemin, Nicolas du, 16th century publisher in Paris, 49, 54ff, 56
Chiaula, Mauro, 1544–1603, composer, 105
Christian III, King of Denmark, 1534–1559, royal wind band library, 24, 57
Christian IV, 1588–1648, of Denmark, 29
Clemens non Papa, Jacques, 1510–1556, Flemish, composer, 25ff, 45, 49, 84, 107ff, 109ff, 114, 118ff, 120, 122ff
Cocq, Gerard de, 16th century composer, 26, 108
Colin, Pierre, 16th century composer, 56
Colombani, Orazio, 1535–1595, composer, 105
Compere, composer in *Odhecaton*, 1501, 17
Conforti, Giovanni, 1560–1608, Italian composer, 96
Conseil, Jean, 1498–1534, French composer, 63
Coprario, John, ca. 1570–1626, English composer, 36
Cordeilles, Charles, fl. 1540–1548 French composer, for Lyons wind band, 56
Cornazzani, Phileno, 1543–1628, lost work for Emperor Ferdinand I, 77
Cornet, Séverin, 1530–1594, Franco-Flemish canzoni, ca. 1563, 121
Cornysh, 16th century composer, 35
Corteccia, Francesco, 1502–1571, Italian composer, 104
Corvinus, Georg, 16th century publisher in Frankfurt, 72
Cosimo de Medici, 104
Cotes, Aambrosio, ca. 1550–1603, Seville, composer, 125
Courtois, Jean, 16th century composer, 26, 63, 119
Cousin, Jean, 1425–1475, Flemish composer, ix
Cowper, 16th century composer, 31, 35
Crequillon, Thomas, 1505–1557, Franco-Flemish composer, 26, 63ff, 82, 84ff, 107ff, 109ff, 117ff, 122ff
Crespel, Jean, fl. mid-16th century, French composer, 26, 107ff, 109, 120, 122ff,
Croce, Giovanni Dalla, 16th century composer, 105
Curtois, 16th century composer, 85

D

D'Auxerre, 16th century composer, 45, 48
Dalla Casa, Girolamo, d. 1601, 1584, *Il Vero Modo de Diminuir*, for wind ensemble, 83, 105
Dalla Casa, Nicoló, d. 1617, Italian composer, 105
Dambert, 16th century composer, , 123
Danckerts (Dankers), Ghiselin, 1510–1565, Dutch composer, 30, 63
Daubmann, Johann, 16th century publisher in Königsberg, 69
Dauxerre, 16th century French composer, 49
Day, J., 16th century publisher in London, 35
De la Rue, 16th century composer, 43
De Latre, Petit Jan, 1505–1569, composer, 26, 107ff, 109, 114, 122ff
Delafont, in 16th century French composer, 45, 48ff
Demantius, Johannes, 1567–1643, German composer, 66
Dentice, Luigi, b. ca. 1510, Naples, composer, 103
Descaudain, 16th century composer, 118
Dietrich, Katharina, 16th – 17th century Nürnberg publisher, 66
Dietrich, Sixt, 1492–1548, composer, 62ff

Domenico, Joan, 16th century composer, 30
Donato, Baldassare, 1525–1603, Italian composer, 65, 114
Donne, Francesco, 1599 publisher in Verona, 93
Dorico, Valerio, 1558 publisher in Rome, 96
Dressler, Gallus, 1533–1590, German composer, 66
Ducis, Benedictus, 1492–1544, German cleric and composer, 27, 62, 65
Dufay, Guillaume, 1400–1474, viiiff, xi

E

Eckel, Mathias, d. 1538, German composer, 27, 62ff
Edwards, 16th century composer in London, 35
Episcopius, Ludovicus, 1520–1595, 107, 114
Erbach, Christian, 1570–1635, German composer, 57, 61
Erban, Johann, Quentels, 16th century publisher in Germany 67
Ercole I d'Este, 1431–1505, Duke of Ferrara, 80
Estrée, Jean, d. 1576, royal oboist and publisher, , 54ff
Evertz, Theodor, mid-16th c. Franco-Flemish composer, 107, 114
Eytelwein, 16th century German composer, 62

F

Faignient, Noel, 1540–1598, Dutch composer, 114
Fayrfax, 16th century English composer, 35
Fèbus, Gaston, 1331–1391 nobleman, 3
Ferber, Augustin, 16th century publisher in Griefswald, 72
Ferrabosco, Alfonso, Jr., 1575–1628, Italian composer, 36
Ferro, Vincenzo, 16th century composer, 30
Festa, Constantio, 1490–1545, Franco-Flemish composer, 27, 38, 44, 48
Fevin, Antonius, 1470–1512, Franco-Flemish composer, 27, 63
Feyerabend, Sigmund, 16th century Frankfurt publisher, 72, 75
Finck, Heinrich, 1444–1527, Franco-Flemish composer, 11, 60, 62ff
Florius, 16th century composer, 107
Fontaine, Pierre, 1380–1450, French composer, viii
Formschneider, H., 16th century publisher in Nürnberg, 61
Forster, Georg, 1515–1568, German composer, 62ff
Franchois, Johannes, fl. ca. 1410–1430, composer, ix
François I, 1515–1547, 37
Frederik II, 1559–1588, of Denmark, 28ff
Fribourg, Henri de, early 15th century (?) composer, ix
Friedrich I of Saxony, 1503–1554, 57
Froissart, 1333–1400, French journalist, 4
Fromschneider, Hieronymus, 16th century German publisher, 62
Frosch, Johann, 16th century German composer, 62ff
Fuchswild, Johann, 16th century German composer, 62
Fugger, John Jacob, 16th century diplomat and businessman, 10
Fugger, R., the elder, owner of 50 ensemble works published in 1523, 106
Fulda, Adam von, 1444–1505, German composer, 61
Füllsack, 17th century publisher in Hamburg, 37

G

Gabrieli, Andrea, 1532–1585, Italian composer, 84ff, 96, 101
Gabrieli, Giovanni, 1553–1612, Italian composer, 86, 96, 103
Galli, Antonio, d. 1565, Italian composer, 107, 109, 123
Gallus, Jacobus, Slovenian composer, 108, 116, 118ff
Ganassi, Silvestro di, b. 1492, Venetian author of treatise on improvisation, 88
Gardane, Antonio, 16th century publisher in Venice, 45, 48ff, 63, 83, 85ff, 89, 92, 94ff, 96ff, 99ff, 102, 104, 121
Geerhart, 16th century composer, 107, 120
Gendre, Le, 16th century composer, 39
Genero, Scipione Vargnanosuo, 1599 publisher in Verona, 93
Geraert, 16th century composer, 108ff
Gerardus (Gerardus Mes), mid-16th c. Franco-Flemish composer, 107, 119ff
Gerlach, Dieterich, 16th century publisher in Nürnberg, 66, 69, 72, 74ff
Gerlach, Katharina, 1580 Nürnberg publisher, 66, 68, 70, 73
Gero, Jhan, fl. 1540–1555, Franco-Flemish composer, 63
Gervaise, Claude, fl. 1540–1560, French composer, 46ff, 50ff
Gesualdo, Carlo, 1561–1613, Italian composer, 104
Gheerkin (Gheerkin de Hondt), d. 1547, Dutch composer, 108
Ghiselin, Jean, late 15th – early 16th c. Franco-Flemish composer, 17, 120
Ghizeghim, Hayne van, 1445–1497, Franco-Flemish composer, 31
Gianotti, Giacomo, fl. 1584, composer, 106
Glanner, Caspar, 16th century German composer, 66
Godard, Robert, 16th c. French organist and composer, 44ff, 49, 109ff
Godart, 16th century composer, 109, 114, 119
Golin, Guilielmo, mid-16th c. composer, 92
Gombert, Nicolas, 1495–1560, Franco-Flemish composer, 27, 38ff, 45, 63, 84, 109ff, 114, 118ff, 122
Goudeaul, in Chemin, N. du, Paris publisher, 45, 49
Grefinger, Wolfgang, 1480–1525, German composer, 61ff
Grossin, Estienne, fl. 1418–1421, French composer, iv, ix
Guami, Giosoffo, 1540–1611, Lucca, composer, 82ff, 91, 104
Guyon, Jean, 16th century composer, 38, 49ff
Guyot, Jean, 1512–1588, Dutch composer, 120, 122
Gwnneth, 16th century composer, 35

H

Hailland, 16th century composer, 107
Hake, John, fl. before 1548, English composer, 35
Hanache, 16th century composer, 120

Hantzsch, Andreas, 16th century publisher in Mühlhausen, 65
Hantzsch, Georg, 16th century publisher in Mühlhausen, 65
Harchadelt, 16th century composer, 44ff
Harelbecanus, Sigerus, 16th century composer, 67
Harnisch, Otto, 16th century composer, 67
Hauricq, 16th century composer, 123
Haussmann, Valentin, 1570–1614, German composer, 67
Havericq, Damien, fl. 1538–1556, composer, 119
Heinrich of Brunswick, 57
Hellinck, Joannes (also known as Lupi, Lupus), 1493–1541, Flemish composer, 27, 63, 114, 120
Henry III, 1551–1589, King of France, ensemble collection 37, 55
Henry IV, 1553–1610, King of France, ensemble collection 37
Henry VIII, 1491–1549, King of England, instrumental works associated with, 31
Hermann, Monk of Salzburg, 1350–1410, 4
Herwich, Christian, 1605–1663, German composer, 78
Hesdin, 16th century composer, 44
Hessen, Paul and Bartholomeus, 16th century composers, 69
Heugel, Johannes, 1500–1585, German composer, 39, 44, 63, 76ff
Heylanus, 16th century composer, 108
Hofhaimer, Paul, 1459–1537, Austrian composer, 23, 61ff
Holborne, Antony, 16th century composer of wind band collection, 33ff, 36ff
Hollande, J., 16th century composer, 118, 120, 122
Hollander, Christian, 1510–1569, Dutch composer, 27, 69, 120
Hollander, Jean, 16th century French composer, 107ff

I

Ingegnieri, Marc'Antonio, 1535–1592, Italian composer, 97
Isaac, Heinrich, 1450–1517, Franco-Flemish composer, 11, 61, 62ff, 65, 106
Isabella d'Este of Ferrara, 15, 80

J

J. S. (Schechinger?), 16th century composer, 62
Jacob, 16th century composer, 107, 109
Jacotin (Godebrye), d. 1529, Flemish composer, 38, 40, 49ff
Jacquet of Mantua, 1483–1559, French composer, 63
Janequin, Clemént, 1485–1558, French composer, 27, 38, 45, 49ff, 63, 85, 107ff, 120, 122ff
Jantian, 16th century composer, 45
Jhan ('Maistre'), 1485–1838, French composer, 63
Jonckers, Goessen, 1500–1555, Belgium composer, 122
Jones, 16th century composer, 35
Jordain, 16th century composer, 107

Josquin, des Prez, 1450–1521 French composer, 17, 26, 63, 107, 119ff

K

Kauffman, Paul, 16th century Nürnberg publisher, 66, 68, 74, 79, 86
Kellnern, Andree, 16th century publisher in Erben, 71
Keutzenhoff, Johannes, German composer ca. 1550, 60
Kilian, 16th century composer, 64
Kirchner, Wolfgang, 16th century publisher in Nürnberg, 66
Knorr, Nicolaus, 16th century publisher in Nürnberg, 70
Kriesstein, M., 1540 German publisher in Augsburg, 63, 76
Kröner, Michael, 16th century publisher in Ülzen, 75
Kugelmann, Johann, 1495–1542, German trumpeter, 76
Kugelmann, Paul, d. 1580, German composer, 69, 77

L

La Rue, Pierre de, 1452–1518, Franco-French composer, 49, 63
Laet, J., publisher in Antwerpen, 1556, 123
Lamberto, 16th century composer, 30
Langenaw, Leonhard von, 16th century German composer, 62ff
Langius, Gregor, 16th century composer, 70
Lapicida, Erasmus, fl. 1510–1521, Franco-Flemish composer, 61ff
Larchier, Joannes, 16th century composer, 27, 61ff, 107, 119ff,
Lasso, Orlando, 1532–1594, composer, 27, 30, 65, 77ff, 85, 109, 118
Lasso, Rudolphum [son of Orlando], 65
Latii, Joanne, 16th century composer, Antwerp, 124
Latins, Arnoldus de, composer, ix
Lauffenberg, Heinrich, 1390–1460, German composer, ix
Layolle, Francesco de, 1492–1540, Florentine composer, 97
Le Cocq, 16th century composer, 107, 108, 118ff
Le Febure, 16th century composer, 65
Le Heurteur, fl. 1530–1545, French composer, 49, 50, 92
Le Jeune, Claude, 1530–1600, Franco-Flemish composer, 107, 108
Le Maistre, Mattheus 16th century composer in Munich, 72
Le moyne, 16th century composer, 43
Le Roy, Adrian, 1520–1598, French composer, 120, 122, 123
Le Roy, Ballard & Patisson, 16th century publishers in Paris, 55
Lebrun, 16th century German composer, 63
Lechner, Leonhard, 1553–1606, Austrian composer, 65, 70, 78
Lemaire, J., 16th century composer, 38
Lemin, 16th century composer, 62, 63
Leo X, 16th century pope, 79
Lescornet, 16th century Franco-French composer, 119

Libero Castro, Henricus de, 1390–1460, Spanish composer, x
Lichtlein, Wilhelm, 16th century German composer, 61
Lindner, Friedrich, fl. 1750–1789 at the Berlin court, German composer, 70
Louis XIII, 1600–1643, King of France, 37
Louys, Jean (Jhan de Loys), 16th century Flemish composer, 107, 108
Lucii (Lucium, Lucius), Jacobi, 16th century publisher in Helmstdt, 61, 67, 72
Lupacchino, Bernardino, 1500–1555 Italian composer, 30
Lupi, Johannes (Jean), 1506–1539, Franco-Flemish composer, 27, 38, 39, 45, 49, 50, 63, 107, 108, 118, 119
Luther, Martin, 73, 78
Lutkeman, Paul, 16th century composer, Wismar, 71
Luzzaschi, Luzzascho, 1545–1607, Italian composer, 97

M

Machinger, 16th century German composer, 62
Magdelain, 16th century French composer, 43, 49
Mahu, Stephen, 1480–1541, Austrian composer, 62, 63, 64
Maillard, Jean, fl. 1538–1572, French composer, 44, 48, 123
Maille, 16th century composer, 45
Mainerio, Giorgio, 1530–1582, Italian composer, 90
Male, Zeghere van 1504–1601, Bruges merchant, owner of ensemble works, 106
Malvezzi, Christofano, 1547–1599, Italian composer, 82, 98
Manchicourt, Pierre, 1510–1564, Franco-Flemish composer, 27, 38, 49ff, 107ff, 118ff
Mancinus, Thomas, 1550–1612, German composer, 72
Marcus, ?, 15th century composer in Florence, 12
Marino, Alessandro, 16th century composer, 98
Marle, Nicolas de, 16th century composer, 49
Maschera, Fiorenzo, 1540–1584, Italian (Brescia) composer, 82, 98
Mathias, 16th century German composer, 63, 64
Maximilian I, 1459–1519, emperor, 11
Mazzi, Luigi, 16th century Ferrara composer, 91
Medici, Giuliano de, ca. 1492–1494, Florence, 16
Meiland, Jakob, 1542–1577, German composer, 72
Meldaert, Leonardo, 1550–1600, composer, , 65
Merulo, Claudio, 1533–1604, Italian composer, 82, 91, 99
Milan, Cornel de, 16th century composer, 27, 108
Millet, 16th century composer, 122
Milliard, 16th century composer, 49
Mittantier, 16th century composer, 44, 49, 50
Modena, Julio da, 1498–1561, composer, 92
Moderne, J., 16th century publisher in Lyon, 46
Molet, 16th century composer, 123
Monte, Filippo de, 1521–1603, Flemish composer, 84, 109
Moreau, Simon, fl. 1553–1558, Franco-Flemish composer, 123
Morel, Jean de, 1511–1581, French composer, 44, 49, 108, 120
Morles, Cristóbal de, 1500–1553, Spanish composer, 63

Mornable, Antoine de, b. ca. 1512, composer, 49
Moscheni, Francesco, 16th century publisher in Milano, 99
Mouton, Jean, 1459–1522, French composer, 27, 63, 118, 119
Mozart, xi
Müllen, van der, 16th century composer, 107
Müller, 16th century German composer, 63

N

Naich, 16th century German composer, 63
Neuber, publisher of 1549 in Nürnberg, , 62
Niccolini, Bernardino, ca. 1465 his wedding music, 14

O

Obrecht, Jacob, 1457–1505, Dutch composer, 8, 106, 107, 108
Ohr, Philipp von, 16th century German composer, 75
Orologio, Alessandre 16th century Italian composer, 61
Othmayr, Casper, 1515–1553, German composer, 60, 63, 64
Otto, Georg, 16th century teacher of Heinrich Schütz, 73

P

Padovano, Annibale, 1527–1575, Venetian composer, 85, 99
Pagnier, 16th century composer, 43
Paminger, Leonard, 1495–1567, German composer, 63, 64
Parabsco, Girolamo, 1524–1577, Italian composer, 94
Parsons, Robert, 1535–1572, English composer, 32, 35
Passereau, Pierre, 1509–1547, composer, 39, 40
Paston, Johan, 1520–1576, Dutch composer, 27
Pathie, Rogier, French composer, 108, 109, 110, 114, 118, 122
Payen, Nicolas, 1512–1559, Franco-French composer, 118
Peetrino, Jacobo, composer, ca. 1583, 124
Peletier, Jacques, 1517–1582, French composer, 45, 63, 92
Pesch, 16th century German composer, 64
Peschin, Gregor, 1500–1547, Slovak composer, 62, 63
Petreius, Johann, 16th century publisher in Nürnberg, 24, 62
Petrucci, Ottaviano, 1501 Venice publisher of *Odhecaton*, 16ff
Petrucci, Pietroiacomo, 1577 publisher in Perugia, 98
Peu d'Argent, Martin, 16th century composer, 84, 108
Phalèse, Pierre, 16th century French publisher in Leuven, 107ff, 110, 114, 124
Philidor, French court wind band collection, 37
Philip of Hesse, ca. 1534–1546, part-books, 59
Phinot, Domenico, 1510–1556, French composer, 27
Pieton, Loyset, fl. 1519–1545, French composer, 118
Pipelare, Matthaeus, 1450–1515, Flemish composer, 9, 61
Poilhiot, 16th century composer, 45
Pontico, Paolo Gottardo, 16th century publisher in Milano, 103
Porta, Constanzo, 1528–1601, Padua, composer, 104
Praetorius, Abraham, 16th century German composer, 74
Praetorius, Christoph, 16th century German, composer, 74ff
Preyz, J. des, 16th century publisher in Langres, 56

R

Rabe, 16th century German composer, 65
Raben, Georg, 16th century publisher in Frankfurt, 75
Rambaldi, Francesco, 16th century Italian composer, 106
Ravel, Sebastiano, 16th century Italian composer, 99
Recourt, 16th century composer, 120
Regiensis, Ambrosius, 16th century German composer, 63
Regnart, Jacob, 1540–1599, Franco-Flemish composer, 73
Regnes, 16th century composer, 43, 49
Rener, Adam, 16th century German composer, 61
Reytter, Oswald, 16th century German composer, 63
Rhau, Georg, 1561 German publisher in Wittenberg, 76
Richafort, Jean, 1480–1547, Franco-Flemish composer, 38, 63, 118, 119
Rogier, Philippe, 1561–1595, Flemish composer, 45, 107
Roquelay, 16th century composer, 49, 50
Rore, Cipriano de, 1516–1565, composer, 27, 83, 85, 89, 92, 107ff, 118ff
Roucourt, Jean-Baptiste, 16th century composer, 118
Ruffo, Vicenzo, 1508–1587, Italian composer, 99

S

Sabbio, Vincenzo, 1584 publisher in Brescia, 99
Sale, ?, fl. ca. 1400, composer, 4
Salmier, Claudius, 16th century composer, 107
Sandrin, Pierre, 1490–1561, composer, 43, 44ff, 49, 50, 52, 109, 110, 114, 118
Scaletta, Orazio, 1550–1630, Italian composer, 101
Scandelli, Luca, 16th century Italian composer, 65
Scandello, Antonio, 1517–1580, composer, 74
Scharffenberg, C., 16th century publisher in Breslau, 64, 69, 70
Schedel, Hartmann, d. 1514, compiled a Liederbuch of 15th century music, 10
Schlegel, 16th century German composer, 65
Schnellinger, 16th century composer, 76
Schonfelder, 16th century German composer, 62
Schramm, Melchior, 1553–1619, German composer, 65, 75
Scotto, Girolamo, 16th century publisher in Venice, 100
Scottum, Hieronymum, 16th century publisher in Venice, 101
Segni, Giulio, 1498–1561, Italian composer, 46
Selneccer, Nicolaus, b. 1539, German composer, 65
Senfl, Ludwig, 1486–1543, German composer, 27, 62, 63, 64, 77
Sermisy, Claudin de, 1490–1562, French composer, 39ff, 43ff, 49ff, 63, 92, 109, 114, 119
Sezza, Gratiano Fido di, 16th century composer, 30
Sezza, Paolo Gigli di, 16th century composer, 30
Shepherd, John, 1520–1563, English composer, 35
Silva, de, 16th century composer, 63
Souliaert, Carolus, d. 1540, Dutch composer, 12
Southerton, Leonard, 16th century English composer, 35
Sponga, Francesco, 1561–1641, Italian composer, 101
St. Julien, Paris wind guild, music of, 37
Stahel, 16th century German composer, 64
Stephen Mahu, 16th century composer, 63
Stivori, Francesco, 16th century composer, 101
Stockaert, Adrien, Flemish, composer, 114
Stoltzer, Thomas, 1480–1526, German composer, 27, 62, 63, 74, 76, 77
Striggio, Alessandro, 1536–1592, Italian composer, 84, 88
Strogers, 16th century composer, 32
Susato, Tielman, 1515–1567, Dutch composer, publisher, 63, 109, 118, 119, 120, 121
Sweelinck, Jan, 1562–1621, Dutch composer, 118
Syringus, Jacobus, 16th century German composer, 75

T

Tallis, Thomas, 1505–1585, English composer, 31, 35
Tavernar, 16th century composer, 35
Tertre, Estienne, 16th century publisher of danceries, 52
Tiburtino, Giuliano, 1510–1569, Italian composer, 101
Tini, Francesco & Simon, 1594 publishers in Milano, 93
Tostolo, Giulian, 16th century composer, 30
Toulouze, ?, publisher before 1496 of basse danse melodies, 18
Touront, Johannes, fl. 1450–1480 composer in Prague, 7
Troiano, M., 16th century Italian singer, 78
Tubal, A., 16th century composer, 27, 108, 123
Turnhout, Gerard de, 16th century Flemish composer, 113, 114
Turnhout, J., 16th century composer, 114
Tye, 16th century composer, 32

U

Unterholtzer, Rupert 16th century composer, 62, 63
Utendal, Alexander, b. 1543, German composer, 65, 75

V

Vaet, Jacob, 1529–1567, Flemish composer, 108, 123
Vala, Do., fl. 1430–1440, composer of wind motet, 'O Thoma Didime', 13
Van der Muelen, 16th century composer, 114
Vassal, 16th century composer, 45
Vecchi, Orazio, 1550–1605, composer, 102
Vencenti, Giacomo, 16th century publisher in Venice, 93, 105
Verbonet, Johannes, 16th century composer, 63
Verdelot, Philippe, 1495–1552, Flemish composer, 63
Verdonck, Cornelis, 1563–1625, Flemish composer, 113, 118
Vermont, Pierre, 16th century composer, 39
Verso, Antonio, 1565–1621, Italian composer, 103
Viadana, Ludovico Grossi da, 16th century composer, 102
Vicentino, Nicoló, 1511–1576, Italian composer, 103
Villiers, Pierre, 1532–1560, Italian composer, 43ff, 49

Vincenzi, Giacomo, 16th century publisher in Venice, 89, 99, 101, 103
Vinci, Pietro, b. 1515, Sicilian composer, 103
Vinders, Hieronymus, composer, 27, 63, 120

W

Waelrant, H., publisher in Antwerpen, 1556, 123
Waelrant, Hubert, 1517–1595, Flemish composer, 27, 107, 108, 114, 123
Walther, Johann, 1496–1570, 27ff, 65, [German Original wind fugues written for Luther] 78
Wannenmacher, Johannes, 1485–1551, Swiss composer, 28, 63
Welack, Matthias, 16th century Wittenberg publisher, 73
Wenck, 16th century German composer, 62
Wend, Johann, 16th century German composer, 75
Wilder, Philip van, 16th century composer, 119, 122
Willaert, Adrian, 1490–1562, Flemish composer, 28, 46, 63, 64, 84, 92, 102, 119, 120, 122
Wintelroy, Jan van, 1520–1576, Franco-Flemish composer, 107, 114
Wismes, Nicholas de, fl. 1554–1564, Dutch comp., 28, 107, 108, 109
Wittel, Martin, 17th century publisher in Erfurt, 70
Wode, Thomas, 16th century composer, 31
Wolcken, Andreas 16th century publisher in Breslau, 66, 68, 70
Wolff, Martin, 16th century German composer, 62

Z

Zaccheus, 16th century composer, 107
Zyrler, Stephen, 16th century German composer, 63

About the Author

Dr. David Whitwell is a graduate ('with distinction') of the University of Michigan and the Catholic University of America, Washington DC (PhD, Musicology, Distinguished Alumni Award, 2000) and has studied conducting with Eugene Ormandy and at the Akademie fur Musik, Vienna. Prior to coming to Northridge, Dr. Whitwell participated in concerts throughout the United States and Asia as Associate First Horn in the USAF Band and Orchestra in Washington DC, and in recitals throughout South America in cooperation with the United States State Department.

At the California State University, Northridge, which is in Los Angeles, Dr. Whitwell developed the CSUN Wind Ensemble into an ensemble of international reputation, with international tours to Europe in 1981 and 1989 and to Japan in 1984. The CSUN Wind Ensemble has made professional studio recordings for BBC (London), the Koln Westdeutscher Rundfunk (Germany), NOS National Radio (The Netherlands), Zurich Radio (Switzerland), the Television Broadcasting System (Japan) as well as for the United States State Department for broadcast on its 'Voice of America' program. The CSUN Wind Ensemble's recording with the Mirecourt Trio in 1982 was named the 'Record of the Year' by The Village Voice. Composers who have guest conducted Whitwell's ensembles include Aaron Copland, Ernest Krenek, Alan Hovhaness, Morton Gould, Karel Husa, Frank Erickson and Vaclav Nelhybel.

Dr. Whitwell has been a guest professor in 100 different universities and conservatories throughout the United States and in 23 foreign countries (most recently in China, in an elite school housed in the Forbidden City). Guest conducting experiences have included the Philadelphia Orchestra, Seattle Symphony Orchestra, the Czech Radio Orchestras of Brno and Bratislava, The National Youth Orchestra of Israel, as well as resident wind ensembles in Russia, Israel, Austria, Switzerland, Germany, England, Wales, The Netherlands, Portugal, Peru, Korea, Japan, Taiwan, Canada and the United States.

He is a past president of the College Band Directors National Association, a member of the Prasidium of the International Society for the Promotion of Band Music, and was a member of the founding board of directors of the World Association for Symphonic Bands and Ensembles (WASBE). In 1964 he was made an honorary life member of Kappa Kappa Psi, a national professional music fraternity. In September, 2001, he was a delegate to the UNESCO Conference on Global Music in Tokyo. He has been knighted by sovereign organizations in France, Portugal and Scotland and has been awarded the gold medal of Kerkrade, The Netherlands, and the silver medal of Wangen, Germany, the highest honor given wind conductors in the United States, the medal of the Academy of Wind and Percussion Arts (National Band Association) and the highest honor given wind conductors in Austria, the gold medal of the Austrian Band Association. He is a member of the Hall of Fame of the California Music Educators Association.

Dr. Whitwell's publications include more than 127 articles on wind literature including publications in Music and Letters (London), the London Musical Times, the Mozart-Jahrbuch (Salzburg), and 39 books, among which is his 13-volume *History and Literature of the Wind Band and Wind Ensemble* and an 8-volume series on *Aesthetics in Music*. In addition to numerous modern editions of early wind band music his original compositions include 5 symphonies.

David Whitwell was named as one of six men who have determined the course of American bands during the second half of the 20th century, in the definitive history, *The Twentieth Century American Wind Band* (Meredith Music).

A doctoral dissertation by German Gonzales (2007, Arizona State University) is dedicated to the life and conducting career of David Whitwell through the year 1977. David Whitwell is one of nine men described by Paula A. Crider in *The Conductor's Legacy* (Chicago: GIA, 2010) as 'the legendary conductors' of the 20th century.

> 'I can't imagine the 2nd half of the 20th century—without David Whitwell and what he has given to all of the rest of us.' Frederick Fennell (1993)

www.ingramcontent.com/pod-product-compliance
Lightning Source LLC
Chambersburg PA
CBHW080551230426
43663CB00015B/2801